Chicken Soup for the Soul®

The Book of

Christmas Virtues

Inspirational Stories
to Warm the Heart

Jack Canfield
Mark Victor Hansen
Carol McAdoo Rehme

Health Communications, Inc.
Deerfield Beach, Florida

www.hcibooks.com
www.chickensoup.com

We would like to acknowledge the following publishers and individuals for permission to reprint the following material. (Note: The stories that are in the public domain, or that were written by Jack Canfield, Mark Victor Hansen or Carol McAdoo Rehme are not included in this listing.)

Homestead Holiday. Reprinted by permission of Margaret Noyes Lang. ©2005 Margaret Noyes Lang.

With Gladness and Glue. Reprinted by permission of Nancy B. Gibbs. ©2000 Nancy B. Gibbs.

Decking the Halls with Balls of Jolly. Reprinted by permission of Gregory S. Woodburn. ©2005 Gregory S. Woodburn.

(Continued on page 189)

Library of Congress Cataloging-in-Publication Data

Chicken soup for the soul : the book of Christmas virtues : inspirational stories to warm the heart / [compiled by[Jack Canfield, Mark Victor Hansen, Carol McAdoo Rehme.
    p. cm.
ISBN-13: 978-0-7573-0314-2 (hard cover)
ISBN-10: 0-7573-0314-5 (hard cover)
ISBN-13: 978-0-7573-0691-4 (trade paper)
ISBN-10: 0-7573-0691-8 (trade paper)
    1. Christmas—Anecdotes. 2. Virtues. I. Title: Book of Christmas virtues.
II. Canfield, Jack, 1944– III. Hansen, Mark Victor. IV. Rehme, Carol McAdoo.

BV45.C545 2005
242'.335—dc22

2005051162

Publisher: Health Communications, Inc.
         3201 S.W. 15th Street
         Deerfield Beach, FL 33442-8190

Cover design by Larissa Hise Henoch
Inside formatting by Lawna Patterson Oldfield

Dedicated to those
who seek
the comfort of home,
the company of friends
and the essence of Christmas.
May you discover it all
within these pages.

Contents

Acknowledgments ix

Introduction: Reflections xiii

Value from Virtues: How to Use This Book...xvii

⭐ Joy

Finders, Keepers 3

Homestead Holiday   *Margaret Lang*...6

With Gladness and Glue   *Nancy B. Gibbs*...10

Decking the Halls with Balls of Jolly   *Woody Woodburn* 12

The Debut   *Mary Kerr Danielson* 15

Music to My Ears   *Margaret Middleton* 18

I Wonder   *Mary Kerr Danielson* 21

Gone Logo 24

⭐ Simplicity

Simply So...27

Tending the Home Fires   *Jim West*...30

Bringing Christmas   *Toby Abraham-Rhine*...33

A Hush in the Rush   *Ann K. Brandt*...36

Whittle-ed A Way   *Carol McAdoo Rehme* 39

Bottomed Out   *Margaret Kirk*..42

Secret Ingredients   *Jane Zaffino*...45

Common Sense 49

⭐ Love

Between the Lines 53

Sweets for the Sweet *Emily Sue Harvey* 56

Nickled and Dimed *Binkie Dussault* 59

Fair Game *James Daigh* 62

Nothin' Says Lovin' Like . . . *Isabel Bearman Bucher* 66

Chords of Love *Margaret Lang* 70

Charlie's Coat *Robin Clephane Steward* 73

Flashing Back *Kathryn Beisner* 77

It's So Lover-ly 80

⭐ Kindness

Mounting Evidence 83

Drawn to the Warmth *Marion Smith* 86

School of "Hire" Learning *Edmund W. Ostrander* 89

Surprise Santa *Henry Boye* 92

In the Bag *Sheila Myers* 94

Stroke by Stroke *Margaret Lang* 98

A Slice of Life *Carol McAdoo Rehme* 101

Sealed with a Kiss 106

⭐ Gratitude

Steeped in Gratitude 109

St. Nick's Note *Pamela Bumpus* 112

Mother to Mother *Annette Seaver* 115

Chilly Today, Hot Tamale *Ellen Fenter* 118

A Piece of Themselves *Carol McAdoo Rehme* 120

Angels and Angst *Sharon Whitley Larsen* 123

It's in the Mail 127

Faith

By Leaps and Mounds...131
Everybody Loves Santa *Robert H. Bickmeyer* 134
Presence and Accounted For *Vickie Ryan Koehler*....................136
Let's Get Real *Charlotte A. Lanham*...138
Ho, Ho, Hope *Angela Hall* 141
Away from the Manger *Stephanie Welcher Thompson*............144
The Family Tree *Carol Keim as told to Tamara Chilla*...............147
Going Global...150

Wonder

Wonder Full 153
A Place of Honor *Mary Kerr Danielson* 156
The Lone Caroler *Bonnie Compton Hanson* 160
The Right Touch *Steve Burt*..162
Christmas Derailed *Armené Humber*..164
Troubled *Woody Woodburn* 167
'Twas the Night *Charlotte A. Lanham*...170
Let It Snow! *Carol McAdoo Rehme*..173
Suitable for Flaming 177

More Chicken Soup? 179
Supporting Others...180
Who Is Jack Canfield?..181
Who Is Mark Victor Hansen? 182
Who Is Carol McAdoo Rehme? 183
Contributors...184
Permissions *(continued)* 189

Acknowledgments

We wish to express our heartfelt gratitude to the following people, who helped make this book possible:

Our families, who have been chicken soup for our souls!

Jack's family, Inga, Travis, Riley, Christopher, Oran and Kyle, for all their love and support.

Mark's family, Patty, Elisabeth and Melanie Hansen, for once again sharing and lovingly supporting us in creating yet another book.

Carol's husband, Norm, whose absolute confidence in her and unfailing support were the backbone of this project. For the many meals he served at her computer—and those he ate alone. For the late nights he kept her company—and the times he didn't. For the gentle critiques he gave when asked—and the opinions he wisely kept to himself. What a guy!

Our publisher Peter Vegso, for his vision and commitment to bringing *Chicken Soup for the Soul* to the world.

Patty Aubery and Russ Kamalski, for being there on every step of the journey, with love, laughter and endless creativity.

Barbara Lomonaco, for nourishing us with truly wonderful stories and cartoons.

D'ette Corona for being there to answer any questions along the way.

Patty Hansen, for her thorough and competent handling of the legal and licensing aspects of the *Chicken Soup for the Soul* books. You are magnificent at the challenge!

Laurie Hartman, for being a precious guardian of the *Chicken Soup* brand.

Veronica Romero, Teresa Esparza, Robin Yerian, Jesse Ianniello, Lauren Edelstein, Jody Emme, Debbie Lefever, Michelle Adams, Dee Dee Romanello, Shanna Vieyra, Lisa Williams, Gina Romanello, Brittany Shaw, Dena Jacobson, Tanya Jones and Mary McKay, who support Jack's and Mark's businesses with skill and love.

Bret Witter, Elisabeth Rinaldi, Allison Janse and Kathy Grant, our editors at Health Communications, Inc., for their devotion to excellence.

Terry Burke, Lori Golden, Kelly Maragni, Tom Galvin, Sean Geary, Patricia McConnell, Ariana Daner, Kim Weiss, Paola Fernandez-Rana, the sales, marketing, and PR departments at Health Communications, Inc., for doing such an incredible job supporting our books.

Tom Sand, Claude Choquette and Luc Jutras, who manage year after year to get our books translated into thirty-six languages around the world.

The art department at Health Communications, Inc., for their talent, creativity and unrelenting patience in producing book covers and inside designs that capture the essence of *Chicken Soup:* Larissa Hise Henoch, Lawna Patterson Oldfield, Andrea Perrine Brower, Anthony Clausi, Kevin Stawieray and Dawn Von Strolley Grove.

All the *Chicken Soup for the Soul* coauthors, who make it

so much of a joy to be part of this *Chicken Soup* family.

Our glorious panel of readers who helped us make the final selections and made invaluable suggestions on how to improve the book.

And most of all everyone who submitted their heartfelt stories and poems, for possible inclusion in this book. While we were not able to use everything you sent in, we know that each word came from a magical place flourishing within your soul.

Because of the size of this project, we may have left out the names of some people who contributed along the way. If so, we are sorry, but please know that we really do appreciate you very much.

We are truly grateful and love you all!

Introduction

Reflections

Holiday greetings, family gatherings, crackling fires, candlelight services, gingerbread men, jingle bells, crunching snow, garlands . . .

What comes to *your* mind when you think about Christmas?

Do you feel excitement? Delight? Wonder? Are you eager to plan, to give, to do? Do you anticipate and participate?

Or do you hallucinate and disintegrate?

Too often, we approach Christmas mired in a puddle of tree lights, fighting to untangle, struggling to straighten things out—the lights, ourselves. We get caught in the clamor of consumerism. We drown in debt.

Worst of all, we forget.

We forget to focus on the pure, unadulterated joy of the season. The kind of wholesome pleasure that seeps into our minds, sneaks onto our lips and slips throughout our souls. That indefinable, unexplainable, indescribable . . . cleansing . . . that washes over us until we are cleaner and clearer, bigger and brighter. Indeed, until we are *better* than ourselves.

And where do we find this elusive *something?*

Within each of us lies the possibility of "better-ness" and the ability to achieve a higher level of moral excellence by adopting virtuous qualities. And what *better* time than Christmas to discover, develop and nurture a virtue?

Christmas, a season of newness, offers us the opportunity for personal renewal. The chance to change ourselves, alter our course, remake our lives. Oh, not necessarily on a grand scale. Small increments—baby steps—will do.

And that is what we offer within the pages of *Chicken Soup for the Soul: The Book of Christmas Virtues*—inspiration to assist your quest for virtue. A collection of stories to encourage retrospection, introspection and quiet reflection.

Our own inspiration comes from the Advent season itself. Perhaps your family, too, reads Scripture and lights candles each Sunday during the month of December, each week focusing on a specific theme. In that same spirit, we selected seven virtues that are symbolic of Christmas: Kindness, Joy, Love, Gratitude, Faith, Simplicity and Wonder. All are characteristics that kindle a light within.

We designed a thought-provoking essay to introduce each virtue and a creative end-of-chapter activity to reinforce it. Then we read through stacks and stacks of stories. Stories that *Chicken Soup* readers—exactly like you—wrote and shared. Stories that depicted the same virtues we chose to emphasize. Stories that encouraged us. Stories that stirred and fired us. Stories that raised us to a higher plane.

From them, we selected the accounts within these pages, anecdotes of all shapes and sizes, exactly like the

people who wrote them. After all, as a wise man once noted, "A human being is nothing but a story with skin around it."

The final product is this treasury of holiday stories, emphasizing the good, the uplifting and the righteous—all without sermonizing. The virtues are evident; the lessons are heartfelt; the journey is one of joy. *The Book of Christmas Virtues* sparkles with the charm of a tinseled tree and crackles with the warmth of a wood-burning stove . . . even as it rings with the familiar voice of home.

Someone once said, "Telling a story is a gift of love." And so, our gift to you this holiday season is in the telling.

Carol McAdoo Rehme

Value from Virtues: How to Use This Book

Use it as a family reader: Take turns reading aloud from it each night. There are enough stories for the entire month of December . . . and more.

Supplement Advent: Pick one of the virtues as your weekly theme, and end each week with the suggested activity.

Use it for holiday teas and luncheons: Share a story or two with the group as entertainment.

Place the book on your coffee table: It is sure to be a constant reminder, year after year, of the true meaning of Christmas.

Give this book as a gift: The only thing better than feeling the holiday spirit is sharing it.

Try the activities: Use these ideas to reinforce your virtues and engage your family.

Joy

Finders, Keepers

Sixty-eight-year-old Ella found it as a volunteer in the newborn nursery at her local hospital: *fulfillment* cuddling her special charge, a new-to-this-Earth preemie whose downy delicacy made her wonder at the fragileness of life.

Up to her elbows in mud, Cassandra noticed it each evening when she straddled her potter's wheel: *mindless ecstasy* in the art of shaping objects of beauty. A quiet bliss in the act of creation itself.

Rebellious and edgy, Natasha felt it seep into her consciousness during her court-mandated community service: *self-satisfaction* in a job well done. A sense of pride she'd never before encountered in her thirteen years.

Ken caught it each time he exchanged his Wall Street suit for his Scout-leader shirt: *jubilation* in the act of pitching camp that he rarely felt on the trading floor. An exuberance as each of his charges mastered a new skill, earned a higher rank and inched a step closer to moral manhood.

José, fresh from massage school, discovered it at the feet of an elderly client: *gratification*—and *humility*—as he kneaded out knots and rubbed her coarse calluses, as he felt her pain-wracked body ease, one tensed muscle after another.

The entire Price family—all eight of them—encountered it the year they "gave away" Christmas: an *elation,* they agreed, greater than any they would have felt had they kept all those gifts for themselves.

So what exactly was it that made these human hearts sing?

Joy. A virtue all of us desire, most of us seek, and each of us would like to claim.

Joy. Such a small, unassuming word—only three letters long—yet often elusive, teasing and winking just beyond our reach.

Joy. What is it? Where can we find it? And . . . how can we keep it?

A veteran fisherman friend put it this way: "Joy works like the bobber on my line; it keeps me from sinking too low." That definition is as plausible and accurate as any a scientist could contrive.

Although we might not be able to easily explain the sensation of joy, we've all witnessed it and—if we're fortunate—experienced it: a kind of happiness-in-action. Sometimes it arrives carbonated—playful, positive and bubbling with festivity. Often, we feel it sneak in—buttoned-up, quiet, satisfying, poignant. And then there's the most expansive brand—with a label that reads *joie de vivre*—that comes bundled with restless curiosity, an appetite for life and a passion for discovery.

No matter how it's packaged, joy is a love song to life. Its lilting melody weaves a harmonious medley of giving, doing, having, being, experiencing and trying. It resonates on notes of optimism, geniality and delight. It feeds your soul.

You'll recognize joy—the famed bluebird of happiness—when you invite it in and offer it a shoulder to perch on.

You can discover it through sacrifice and service or in creativity and purpose. You can find it in tender moments and in exhilarating events. You might recognize it in the promise of a day's dawning or the satisfaction of twilight's final nod.

But is it possible to hold on to that sense of joy? Of course. Although joy is often described as fleeting, it is possible to create it again and again. George Bernard Shaw once proclaimed, "The joy in life is to be used for a purpose. And I want to be used up when I die."

So invest yourself in a purpose this holiday season: your time, your energy, your talents, your emotions. Spend yourself freely . . . and discover joy.

Homestead Holiday

I had so wanted to celebrate Christmas at the two-hundred-year-old farmhouse, surrounded by the love of the dear relatives who had labored to preserve it. A delightful throwback to an era of simplicity—no phones to jangle nerves, no electric lights to glare in eyes—the place veritably shouted, *"Christmas!"* But first things first; we had to settle in.

"Let's make it easier for our folks to get up," I said to my cousins on our first morning at the old homestead.

We drew well water in tall buckets and carried split logs chin high. Soon a kettle whistled on the cast-iron stove. In each bedroom, we poured warm water into the pitchers of porcelain wash sets.

Our efforts paid off. Our sleepy-eyed parents climbed out of Victorian beds to chat over cinnamon rolls and coffee.

We girls cranked the Victrola in the parlor and pedaled the empty spinning wheel in the hall. Everything about this place was a novelty. We read century-old magazines in

the barn and memorized epitaphs in the family cemetery.

We bathed in the fresh waters of Connor Pond and shared teen secrets on the two-holers at "the end of the line." We purchased a block of ice for the antique box in the shed and even scrubbed down the "Grouch House" for would-be guests.

But we wanted so much more.

We wanted Christmas!

"It might be a little odd," one cousin said.

"Sure would," echoed the other.

"Let's ignore that," I said.

Cross-legged on the antique bed in our upstairs hide-away, we plotted how we could pull it off.

"We'll handcraft decorations for the tree," said one cousin.

"We'll pick up gifts in the village . . . even a holiday meal," chimed the other.

"And we'll send out invitations," I said.

The wide plank flooring quivered under our combined energy.

On stationery found in the parlor desk, we composed rhymed couplets penned in our best script. Convinced Keats would be proud, we lost no time in posting them.

We begged our moms to pick up a few items at the grocery store—okay, maybe not a turkey, but how about a holiday brunch with eggs Benedict and a fresh fruit cup? "And don't forget maple syrup for waffles!"

We popped corn in a pan and strung garland, yet so much was missing. There were no ornaments to be found anywhere. We poked through brush along a New England stone wall and fell upon a treasure trove of cones, seed-pods and nuts. We tied loops around red-berry sprigs and

green crabapple stems. Scissors soon fashioned white
paper into snowflakes and tinfoil into a star.

Thoughts of the tree encouraged us—but the mailbox
didn't. Every afternoon, we rode down the mountain to
check it. Still no reply to our invitations—even though the
event was upon us.

On the morning of the anticipated day, our folks dis-
tracted us with an excursion to the mountains. We arrived
home late and tired.

Dad went in first to light the kerosene lamps. When the
windows were aglow, we girls ambled upstairs. We
stopped at the sound of bells.

"What is it?" I craned over the stairwell.

"Ho, ho, ho," resounded in the distance.

"It's *got* to be Chesley!" Dad said, lamp in hand, as he
peered out the front door into the darkness.

Chesley and Barbara, I thought. *The guests are arriving!*

I jumped down the stairs in time to see a fully regaled
Santa leap into the lamplight. A prim Mrs. Claus joined
him by the house.

"You didn't think it was a dumb idea, after all!" we girls
shouted.

"Oh, we thought it was wonderful," they said.

Such gameness of spirit spurred us cousins to action.
We chopped down a forest fir, placed it in the sitting room
and smothered it with our handmade treasures.

Before the crackling fire in the hearth, Mrs. Claus
rocked while Santa distributed our carefully selected gifts.

Chocolate mints, knickknacks and a dainty handkerchief . . . even Roy Tan cigars for Dad.

The impossible had actually happened: a farmhouse Christmas . . . *in August!*

True, this was a most uncommon New Hampshire Christmas. Instead of frost nipping at our toes, perspiration beaded our foreheads. Rather than windows iced shut, fragrant breezes blew past. In place of quietly falling snow, a chorus of crickets performed. Where snowsuits would have hung, swimsuits dried on pegs.

Yet the love of celebrating, which knew no season, abounded. And therein lay the joy.

Margaret Lang

With Gladness and Glue

While Christmas shopping in a jewelry store, I discovered a clearance table of gilded ornaments. Detailed and delicate in design, each had a personality all its own. I sorted among the hundreds of filigreed masterpieces, picked out a few and took them home.

Deciding they were much too pretty to disappear among the clutter of a Christmas tree, I used them instead to decorate small eight-inch wreaths. When I stood back to admire my handiwork, a thought crossed my mind: *Wouldn't some of our family and friends like these, too?*

I raced back to the jewelry store to discover that the stack of ornaments had been reduced even further. This time I bought dozens as I thought of the many people who might enjoy one for the holidays.

Armed with a glue gun and bright ribbons of every color, I eagerly began my creative project. The wreaths multiplied like measles and dotted every flat surface in our house. For days, my family tiptoed around, elbowed their way through and slept among the miniature masterpieces.

While I tied dainty bows and glued golden ornaments, my mind wandered to Christmases past, and I pondered how special each had been. I thought about others perhaps not so fortunate. Some people in our community didn't have a family to share the joy of Christmas. Some didn't bother with holiday decorations. Some never left their homes to celebrate the season.

I nodded my head in determined satisfaction. They would be at the top of my list to receive a little wreath. My husband joined me in the plan, and we set out together to put it into action.

We visited the aged. We visited the widowed. We visited the lonely. Each one was thrilled with our cheery stops and immediately hung our small gifts—often the only signs of celebration in their homes.

After several days, I realized we had made and given almost two hundred wreaths. Decorated with love and delivered with delight, they filled many homes and hearts with the joy of Christmas.

And I came to the simple realization that *we* were actually the ones who received the greatest blessing that year. We had found *our* Christmas spirit in the doing.

Nancy B. Gibbs

Decking the Halls with Balls of Jolly

A number of years ago, NBA All-Star Cedric Ceballos hosted a free basketball clinic for a couple hundred young-sters. At the end of the event, Ceballos—then playing for the Los Angeles Lakers—handed out half a dozen auto-graphed basketballs.

One lucky recipient, a boy about eleven years old, hugged Ceballos and then hugged the ball. But what really touched me was this: As I left the gym, I saw the boy outside shooting baskets on one of the blacktop courts . . . using his autographed ball.

While the other handful of lucky kids surely went home and put theirs in places of honor, this boy had already dribbled, shot and worn off Ceballos's valuable signature.

Curious, I asked the boy why he hadn't taken the ball straight home.

"I've never had my own ball to shoot with before," he explained happily.

It made me wonder about similar kids—kids who don't have their own basketballs to shoot, their own soccer balls to kick, their own footballs to throw or their own baseballs to play catch. And so it was that I began using my regular sports column to ask readers to step up to the plate. I started an annual ball drive for underprivileged children.

Great gifts, with no batteries required and no breakable parts.

The first year, about one hundred were donated. That just got the ball rolling, so to speak. The next year's total was 363, then 764 and 877.

Which brings us to this past Christmas. And Briana.

After reading my Thanksgiving Day column announcing "Woody's Holiday Ball Drive," Briana responded like an All-Star point guard. The nine-year-old dished out assists like a mini–Magic Johnson. In notes attached to her generous gifts for other kids, she wrote, in neat printing that would make her teacher proud, a message that should make her parents even prouder:

> *I saw your wish list in the paper and I wanted to help. I know how important it is to help others. So this year I saved money by collecting recycables (sic). So here I give to you: 5 basketballs, 2 footballs, 2 soccer balls, 1 volleyball, 1 bag of baseballs, 1 bag of softballs. I hope this helps.*
>
> *Happy holidays,*
> *Briana Aoki*

Her generosity kicked off a heartwarming campaign of kids helping kids in need.

As a result, ten-year-old Sarah and eight-year-old Mitch emptied "The Jar." Kept on the family's fireplace hearth, it collected pocket change, some chore money and even coins found in the laundry. Sarah chose a soccer ball and Mitch selected a football to buy and share.

Professional tennis players Mike and Bob Bryan, identical twins, served up a donation of twenty-five footballs and one hundred top-of-the-line basketballs. Others stepped forward, too.

The life lesson here is this: A lot of great kids find joy in giving and joy in sharing—loose change in a jar, wages for chores, allowance money, coins from recycling—just to make a difference. A big difference. A difference of . . .

397	basketballs
218	footballs
178	playground balls
161	soccer balls
104	baseballs
29	softballs
26	cans of tennis balls
14	volleyballs

GRAND TOTAL: 1,127 balls—and smiles
—for kids in need this
Christmas morning.

Woody Woodburn

The Debut

"Mom, where's the roll of butcher paper?" JoAnn asked as she rummaged in the kitchen drawer for scissors and tape. Off she trotted down the hall, clasping the items.

Gathered for our family Christmas party, all three generations had finished eating. Now, the little cousins eagerly left parents and grandparents behind to begin preparations for the annual nativity pageant. Sequestered in the far recesses of the house, the youngsters plotted behind closed doors.

Grateful for peace and quiet, we adults basked in the festive glow of the fire, nibbled remnants of our delicious dinner and continued chatting. We felt no need to hurry our budding geniuses, tickled that they found delight in planning this project together.

An occasional burst of dialogue erupted through the open door as first one then another child was dispatched on a crucial errand. A jar of craft paint, then a wide paintbrush disappeared into their inner sanctum. Intense forays commenced throughout the house as armloads of

towels, bathrobes, scarves, bed sheets, belts and jewelry joined their stash. Giggles and whispers intensified as their conspiracy continued.

We knew the project must be coming together when they mounted an intense search for bobby pins, large safety pins, paper clips, even clothespins—anything to hold costumes and props in place. Everyone's anticipation heightened as the cast and crew finished their preparations.

When the designated spokesperson called for our attention, a hush fell over the room.

Two stagehands wrestled a long, butcher-paper poster and, with copious lengths of tape, secured it to the wall. Emblazoned in bright paint it read:

Bethlehem Memorial Hospital

The makeshift stage became a busy reception area of the hospital. One bossy cousin greeted newcomers, summoned aides and kept employees scurrying. Instead of halos, "nurse-angels" wore folded-paper caps with red painted crosses. They assessed each case, wielding their make-believe stethoscopes and thermometers before sending patients off to imaginary treatments.

Mary, endowed with a plump throw pillow, entered, leaning on Joseph's sturdy arm for support. Rejected by the insensitive innkeeper, they found a warm welcome at Bethlehem Memorial where one escort whisked Mary off to delivery and another led Joseph to the waiting room.

Joseph paced; he wrung his hands; he nodded off while shuffling through old magazines. He begged for the latest

news on Mary's condition. At proper intervals, a nurse appeared with an encouraging, "It won't be long now."

After our young thespians had milked the scene dry, unseen hands shoved the last performer onto the stage.

There stood Connie Beth, the youngest nurse-angel in the troupe. Her scrap of angel robe in disarray, her nurse cap askew, she inched toward Joseph. Having outgrown her role as babe-in-the-manger, this year—oh, joy—she had a speaking part.

Suddenly aware of her audience, Connie Beth froze. She ducked her head, lowered her eyes and studied the floor. Her tongue probed the inside of her cheek and lower lip. A tiny finger crept toward her mouth. The toe of her little tennis shoe bore into the carpet fibers.

Would stage fright be her undoing?

Offstage, a loud whisper shattered the silence. "Tell Joseph about the baby!"

Connie's head lifted. Her countenance brightened. Resolve replaced fear.

She hesitated, searching for the right words. Taking a deep breath, she stood before Joseph and quietly delivered her joyous message:

"It's a girl!"

Mary Kerr Danielson

Music to My Ears

I sat silently in the backseat as we drove home from an evening church program where I'd heard once again the wondrous story of Jesus' birth. And my heart flooded with happiness as the three of us hummed to familiar Christmas carols drifting from the car radio.

With my nose pressed against the side glass, I gawked at the department-store displays. As we passed houses with lighted Christmas trees in the windows, I imagined the gifts piled under them. Holiday cheer was everywhere.

My happiness lasted only until we came to the gravel road leading to our home. My father turned onto the dark country lane where the house sat two hundred yards back. No welcoming lights greeted us; no Christmas tree glowed in the window. Gloom seeped into my nine-year-old heart.

I couldn't help but wish for trees and presents like other children. But the year was 1939, and I was taught to be grateful for the clothes on my back and the shoes on my feet, to be thankful for a home—no matter how

humble—and for simple food to fill my growling belly.

More than once, I'd heard my folks say, "Christmas trees are a waste of money."

I guessed gifts must be, too.

Although my parents had climbed out of the car and gone into the house, I lingered outside and sank down on the porch steps—dreading to lose the holiday joy I'd felt in town, wishing for Christmas at *my* house. When the late-night chill finally cut through my thin dress and sweater, I shuddered and wrapped my arms around myself in a hug. Even the hot tears streaking down my cheeks couldn't warm me.

And then I heard it. Music. And singing.

I listened and looked up at the stars crowding the sky, shining more brightly than I'd ever seen them. The singing surrounded me, uplifting me. After a time, I headed inside to listen to the radio where it was warm.

But the living room was dark and still. How odd.

I walked back out and listened again to the singing. Where was it coming from? Maybe the neighbor's radio? I padded down the long road, glorious music accompanying me all the way. But the neighbor's car was gone, and their house was quiet. Even their Christmas tree stood dark.

The glorious music, however, was as loud as ever, following me and echoing around me. Could it be coming from the other neighbor's house? Even at this distance, I could plainly see no one was there. Still, I covered the three hundred yards separating their house and ours.

But there was nothing and no one.

Yet to my ears the singing rang clear and pure. To my

eyes the night stars shone with such radiance that I wasn't afraid to walk home alone. Once I reached my house, I sat again on the porch steps and pondered this miracle. And it *was* a miracle. For I knew in my young heart and soul I was being serenaded by the angels.

I was no longer cold and sad. Now I felt warm and happy, inside and out. As I gazed upward into eternity, surrounded by the praise of heavenly hosts, I knew I had received a joyous Christmas gift after all—a gift straight from God.

The gift of love.

The shining star.

And an everlasting Christmas.

Margaret Middleton

I Wonder

I wonder if that precious babe
were born somewhere today,
Would he recline on Bubble-Pak®
instead of straw or hay?

Would the message of the angel
be broadcast on TV—
Just one more televangelist
ignored by you and me?

Would the anthems of that heavenly choir
hit Nashville from the start?
With concerts, tapes and CDs,
no doubt they'd climb the charts.

Would we confuse that glowing star
with satellites in space,
Or think it just a UFO
from a distant, cosmic place?

The "Jesus news" would travel fast
in this Information Age—
By phone, by fax, by e-mail,
perhaps his own Web page.

Would we gladly leave our tasks behind
and travel far and wide,
Not hesitating in our quest
to worship at his side?

The answer lies within each soul.
Each year we get to choose
How we will celebrate his birth
and greet the wondrous news.

He comes! He comes! (though not a babe)
so softly none can hear,
And creeps into your life and mine
this joyous time of year.

And listen. Oh, just listen,
his sounds are all around—
The choir's song, the call of friends,
snow crunching on the ground.

The laughter of the children,
the ringing of each bell,
The stories and the carols
we've learned to love so well.

So pause amid the craziness,
embrace each mem'ry dear.
Let tastes and smells and sights and sounds
delight nose, eyes and ears.

And welcome him this holiday
with laughter and with joy,
His gift of hope, his gift of life,
That blessed, holy boy.

Mary Kerr Danielson

Gone Logo

Customize Christmas by proclaiming *your* personal "joy to the world."

Purchase a rubber stamp that reads "Joy," along with colored inkpads, from a stationery or scrapbook supply store—or have one custom designed at a local printing firm.

Stamp butcher paper, tissue paper or brown paper for gift wrap. Embellish plain white or colored gift bags. And don't forget to create coordinating gift tags.

Use the stamp to personalize your holiday cards, stationery, envelopes, thank-you notes and address labels. What about decorating paper napkins, tablecloths, place cards and nametags? And don't forget to stamp each bill you pay!

Make "joy" your logo this year, and spread it freely.

Simplicity

Simply So

Too often, December arrives shrink-wrapped in good intentions. Big plans, high hopes—and wishful thinking.

We envision a Norman Rockwell holiday that crackles with the toe-melting warmth of an old-fashioned, wood-burning fire. Or a Martha Stewart holiday that sparkles with fine crystal, heirloom china and polished silver reflecting the romantic glow of gilded candlelight. Or a Lawrence Welk holiday that rings with the eager excitement of mittened children, the familiar laughter of old friends and the lilting songs of muffler-wrapped carolers.

We envision a holiday that simmers the flavors of mulled cider, clove-studded oranges, hand-dipped chocolates and homey yeast breads. That glitters with the charm of wreathed doors, bulb-frosted eaves and tinseled trees. A Christmas piled high with parcels, packages and presents—handpicked, handmade, hand wrapped.

Signed.

Sealed.

Delivered.

We expect to achieve it all—all at one time, all in one month, all in one breath—often at the expense of the people and things we hold even more dear. And we rarely allow ourselves time to smell the poinsettias.

But there is an alternative. A simpler Christmas, a more novel Noel. We can scale back in order to really "savor the season." Instead of trying to do so much, what if we focus on the traditions we value and eliminate the rest?

Consider making a personal list of your typical holiday activities. Include everything from addressing greeting cards to sewing matching red pajamas to unpacking crates of decorations. Think about each item.

What makes your children groan?

What makes *you* groan?

Are there any particular activities your family has *out*grown?

What could be done during another season instead? (Perhaps opting to decorate sugar cookies for Valentine's Day or waiting to mail annual newsletters as a New Year's Day event.)

How can some activities be simplified? (Maybe donating to charities in lieu of gift giving, shopping via the Internet to avoid the mall throngs or entertaining in the post-Christmas lull rather than at the height of the season.)

Now, make a second list of holiday activities you *wish* you could do. It might mention things like romping in a new snow or curling up to reread the old, familiar Christmas story—straight from the Bible. Participating in the community's resounding rendition of Handel's "Hallelujah Chorus" or leisurely lunching with a dear friend. Playing the role of robed shepherd in a live nativity or sipping nutmeg-freckled eggnog in front of the fire. Watching *How the Grinch Stole Christmas* with the whole family or taking a solitary walk under a star-studded sky. Attending a local charity event with your spouse or stringing popcorn and cranberries with the grandkids.

Prioritize the items you've *chosen* to keep with those you've decided to *add*. Be certain there is a healthy balance between self, family and others. Above all, see to it that your list is short. Compact. Simple.

Now, slow down and enjoy each event. Savor it to the fullest. Linger over it. Then—learn to linger longer.

And tuck this among the gifts you give yourself and your loved ones this year: *simplicity.*

Tending the Home Fires

Our hardworking parents always did their best to provide memorable holidays for their family of seven.

Weeks before Christmas, my father pulled double and even triple shifts at the cement mill to make sure there would be presents under the tree. Coated in ashes and soot, he'd drag into the house each night, bone-weary from cleaning out smokestacks. Besides one full-time job as city clerk and another one mothering us, Mom did all the things necessary back in the 1960s to make our budget stretch: sewing clothing into the wee hours of the morning, mending hand-me-downs, packing school lunches and laundering cloth diapers.

Even so, my parents emphasized the memory-making moments: designing elaborate macaroni ornaments to decorate the tree, hanging dozens of cheery greeting cards from loved ones around our bedroom doorframes, and singing carols as we hauled aging boxes of decorations from the basement to the living room. In mid-December, Mom gathered her baking sheets, her huge wooden rolling

pin and her kids to spend an entire day in the cramped kitchen baking and decorating sugar cookies.

And she always delegated one duty to me.

Because our scant living room had no fireplace to hang stockings, we used a cardboard-kit substitute. It was my job to assemble it each year, that special place where Santa would soon leave his few presents for us.

Against one wall, I unfolded the fireplace front. Then I placed and balanced the black cardboard mantle that bore wounds from dozens of punctures where we'd thumb-tacked our stockings during holidays past. After I inserted a red lightbulb into the hole near the metal spinner, I plugged in the cord so the logs would "burn."

Satisfied at last, I settled to the floor in my favorite nook across from the fireplace—directly in front of a furnace vent. I knew the warm air blew from the basement, but in my mind, the heat spread from the cardboard logs to ignite my imagination. It was there that I spun my boyish dreams and lived my foolish fantasies.

The years drifted on, and so did I.

When all of us kids were grown and on our own, our parents hit the jackpot. I mean, *really* hit the jackpot. In a big way. They won over two million dollars in the Illinois State Lottery!

As instant millionaires, the first thing they did was look for a new place to live. My father insisted on only two musts: an attached garage and . . . a working fireplace. My mom wanted more space. And they found it: a beautiful two-story house with four bedrooms, a spacious kitchen, a dining area, a two-car garage, a roomy basement—and a living room with a working fireplace.

In December after their move, we all came home for our first holiday together in years. While everyone lazed and chatted by the fireside on Christmas Eve, I rose to my feet to stroll through the house on a private tour.

Mom had decorated with recently purchased crystal ornaments and a hand-carved Santa from Germany. Embroidered holiday doilies graced new end tables, and expensive wrapping paper enveloped dozens of presents under the beautifully lit tree. From top to bottom, the place murmured, *"New. Gorgeous. Tasteful."* It certainly wasn't home as I remembered it.

Near the stairwell, I glanced up . . . and did a double take. Perched at the top, like a forgotten old friend I might bump into on the corner, stood the raggedy cardboard fireplace. With a smile as wide as Mom's rolling pin, I climbed the stairs and sank to the top step as a wave of boyhood memories washed over me.

Before long, Mom found me upstairs and stood silently at my side. I looked up, waiting for her eyes to meet mine.

"You kept it, this old fireplace in your new home. Why?"

After a long moment, she placed her hand on my shoulder and bent toward me. "Because I don't ever want any of us to forget the simple joys of Christmas," she whispered.

And I nodded in understanding, pleased that I could still feel the warmth radiating from the old, cardboard fireplace.

Jim West

Bringing Christmas

Some of life's events make permanent etchings on your soul.

Like the Christmas our family spent volunteering with the people of Santisimo Sacramento. Situated in the heart of Piura, Peru, this church was the lifeblood of the thirty-three thousand citizens it served. We spent long, hot days sorting and distributing clothes, tearing down and rebuilding a house, fixing donated bikes and becoming part of the community.

I don't even have to close my eyes to remember endless sand dotted with scraggly trees, the truck's horn competing with mangy, barking dogs, the smell of heat and sweat, and the gritty taste of dirt roads. And the children. Hundreds of big-eyed, bronze-skinned, dark-haired children chasing after us with the hope of youth.

Several times a day, bouncing along sand and gravel, we all struggled to hold on to the sides of the white pickup truck, laughing so hard that our smiles petrified above our wind-dried teeth. Ginet, our driver, laid on the horn with the jubilation of Robin Hood delivering goods to the poor, while villagers ran from all corners of the surrounding pueblos.

Our three children—Clare, Bridget and Michael—helped prepare barrels of chocolate milk and hundreds of buttered rolls for distribution in the villages and the prison.

One afternoon, we pulled up to a small, dusty church, skirted the ever-present dogs and rearranged rickety wooden benches on the cement floor. One hundred fifty children sat patiently, each with a cup brought from home, to receive the coveted treat. Mothers remained in the doorway, watching as their children participated in prayer and songs before they were served chocolate milk and a buttered roll.

Finally, each child received a token toy. In less than twenty minutes, their Christmas had come . . . and gone.

We trucked through the pueblo, distributing more toys. One tiny girl ran after us for a good two hundred yards. When she finally reached the driver's side door, she was ecstatic to receive a small toy. As we drove on, an older girl grabbed the gift and left her sobbing among the crowd.

Distressed, at the next stop we explained what had happened and asked Ginet to drive back and search the village. At last, Clare and Bridget spotted the child outside her shack, still crying. When we replaced the toy, her smile was jubilant.

Naturally, questions haunted us during our stay:

How should we handle Christmas with our own children?

Would they expect gifts on Christmas morning?

Surrounded by such poverty, could we justify our giving and receiving?

As Steve and I pondered the situation and faced our choices, we couldn't help making comparisons between these different cultural traditions.

We saw Christmas in Peru celebrated so simply—with *Las Posadas* to commemorate the journey of Mary and Joseph, bonfires, *panettone* (Italian bread) and *leche de chocolate* (hot cocoa). There were no Christmas trees, no gifts exchanged and no Santa Claus. The *only* reason for the season was the Holy Family and Christ's birth. The focus was clearly on people, relationships and doing for others.

What greater gift could we give our own children?

In the end, we presented each with a tiny finger harp from Kenya and a small token from Santa. As a family, we spent Christmas morning writing down what we hoped for each other. Those scraps of paper and their thoughtful words remain priceless to this day, and our children still revel in the memory of that humble celebration.

We had gone to volunteer and bring Christmas to the poor. Instead, the villagers of Piura brought a richer, deeper sense of Christmas to *us*—Christmas without the trappings.

Toby Abraham-Rhine

A Hush in the Rush

I always began December with Big Plans: baking ten kinds of cookies, decorating the house creatively and entertaining lavishly.

One bright morning in early December, while butter softened for the press cookies and yeast grew in sugar and water, the telephone rang. My recently widowed friend needed to talk. An hour passed. The butter melted; the yeast spilled over the bowl. And the clock was ticking. We chatted a bit longer, and her mood lightened as we made plans to meet.

A voice inside reminded me, *Christmas is, after all, about generosity.*

Our lunch the next day lasted longer than I anticipated, and snail-paced traffic slowed my trip home. When a car cut into my lane, a flash of anger almost kept me from seeing the old man waiting to cross the street. I braked to a stop and motioned him on.

Patience, whispered the inner voice, *allow time for kindness.*

While I rushed to wash my front windows before decorating them, an elderly neighbor threw a sweater over her shoulders and came over to pass the time. It got lonely, she confided, with her son and his wife at work all day. Reluctantly, I set aside the spray cleaner and the rags.

"Would you like to come in for a cup of tea?" I heard myself asking.

Ah, I heard the voice say, *you're getting the idea.*

Armed with a lengthy master list, I hurried off on the grim task of shopping. After an exhausting battle with crowds in overheated stores, I emerged triumphant and smug. Outside the mall, bell ringers shivered in the blowing snow, and I felt compelled to pull out my last bill for their plump kettle.

"Thank you, ma'am! Merry Christmas!"

I see you're learning sacrifice, too, the voice praised.

Later in the week, my daughter called long-distance, desperate for a heart-to-heart talk. I glanced at the unwrapped presents strewn across the floor. I looked at my watch. And back at the piles. Then I remembered the loneliness and isolation and frustration of young motherhood—and settled in the overstuffed chair for a long, leisurely chat.

"Check back with me again this afternoon," I said, "so I'll know how you're getting along." I tossed another look at the presents and shrugged.

The gift of your time, I heard, *is the best gift of all.*

The Sunday before Christmas, our still-bare tree leaned against one corner of the living room.

"We should've bought a new tree stand. The tree is top heavy, and this one won't hold it," my husband groaned.

Ignored in my holiday rush, he looked tired and lonely with his rumpled gray hair, worn jeans and untucked shirttail—this man who was as much a part of my life as my own body.

I reached out and touched his rough cheek. "I'll help with the tree."

Good, said the inner voice, *you've remembered the love.*

Throughout the afternoon, we pruned and sawed. We got out ornaments accumulated and treasured throughout the long years of our marriage. And when the tree was trimmed, I made hot chocolate and served it in the little pot we first used so many Christmases ago.

On Christmas day, our children arrived, and the house rocked with laughter, conversation, grandbabies and music.

No one noticed the smears on the window where decorations hung askew or the branches missing from one side of the tree. No one cared that dinner was a potluck affair. No one commented on the lack of variety on the cookie tray.

But when I brought out a simple cake with one glowing white candle, the room hushed. Every one of us—wide-eyed children and solemn adults—held hands while we sang "Happy Birthday" to Jesus.

A feeling of contentment welled up inside me that had nothing to do with cookies, clean windows or fancy wrappings.

And that still, small voice said, *Yes!*

Ann K. Brandt

Whittle-ed Away

"Connie Ann!" Mom caught the piece of tinfoil in midair. "We might need this next time we bake potatoes. You know better than that."

Ashamed, Connie Ann gave a gusty, seven-year-old sigh and retreated from the kitchen. Yes, she knew better. The Whittle family creed demanded that everything, even a piece of foil, be used again . . . and again. Especially now, with the divorce and all.

And she knew about other things, too. Like salvaging buttons and zippers from old clothes to use on the new ones her mom sewed. Like gagging on dust clouds each time someone emptied the vacuum bag instead of throwing it away. Like walking everywhere when most of her friends rode in cars. Of course, the Whittles didn't own a car; Dad had left them the Pumpkin.

The bronzey colored, short-bed pickup couldn't hold all ten children at once, so the Whittle children walked. To school. To church. To get a gallon of milk. Mom said it was

simpler than buying a car. Besides, they got exercise and saved on gas at the same time.

Mom said she liked doing things the simple way. In fact, that's how she got rid of the Christmas tree, too.

Without Dad there to haul it out that year, she puzzled over the problem. "How will we get rid of this monstrosity?"

She circled the tree.

"It seems like a waste to just throw it away. It should be good for something, shouldn't it?"

Connie Ann nodded in agreement, knowing Whittles never wasted *anything*.

"It still smells good." Mom poked both arms through the brittle needles to heft its weight. *"Hmmm."* Her brow furrowed a bit, and she glanced over her shoulder where coals still glowed in the fireplace.

"Our gas bill has been sky high." She scooted the tree from its nook in front of the window. "If I just push it in . . . a bit at a time . . . as it burns. . . ." She wrestled the tree to the floor.

"Connie Ann, you grab that end while I drag the bottom."

Wincing from the pain and prickles of the browning evergreen, they struggled to get their handholds.

"What could be simpler?" Mom half-shoved it across the floor with a grunt. "A fragrant room freshener," she tugged at the trunk, *"and* free heat," she gave one final push, *"and* we get rid of this thing."

With a precise aim, she poked the tippy-top of the tree right into the middle of the glowing embers.

KA-VOOOOM!

In a roar as loud as a sonic boom, the entire tree—from its bushy head to its board-shod feet—burst into one

giant flame. Screaming, Mom dropped the trunk, and they both jumped across the room.

WHOOOOSH!

All the branches disappeared. In one big breath. Just like magic. Nothing was left of the Christmas tree except a charred trunk, some scraggly Charlie Brown twigs—and a trailing, tree-shaped shadow of white ashes.

For one long, bug-eyed moment, Mom caught her breath. Then she pulled Connie Ann close to search for burns and swept a glance over herself for singes. And she examined the carpet for damage. Finding none, she slowly shook her head in wonder.

After a stunned silence, Mom brushed her hands together efficiently. "Well! I guess that takes care of that."

Then she picked from among the newly formed crowd of wide-eyed, jabbering children.

"You and you and you," Mom pointed at the oldest, "help me haul this tree outside. At least *now* it's manageable."

Connie Ann nodded in agreement. She knew how much Mom liked things kept simple. It was, after all, the Whittle way.

Carol McAdoo Rehme

Bottomed Out

It was a difficult week.

He had completed some work in exchange for the promise that "the check is in the mail." *Not.* Only bills appeared in his mailbox and never a check to pay them.

It was the holiday season—with its own slew of stressors—and the car was on the fritz again, the larder was frightfully empty, and his regular payday wasn't until the end of the month. No food. No money. No hope.

For certain, he'd hit the bottom of the barrel.

What was he going to do? Teetering on the brink of despair, he took three deep breaths, reached for his overcoat, scarf and gloves, and headed toward the woods. Nature had always been the sanctuary he sought when he felt hopeless or depressed.

Accommodating his stride to the snow-covered ground, he crunched through the forest of regal pines and snow-flocked blue spruce. He shaded his eyes against brilliant sunlight where it mirrored the diamond-bright snow. The tip of his nose reddened, and his cheeks burned from the crisp air.

As he headed toward the pond backing his property, a deer bounded across the path. A more timid tufted titmouse followed from a distance.

And he felt his breathing gentle and his gait slow.

"Chickadee-dee-dee!" A vigilant warbler sounded its alarm. A crow flitted from treetop to fence post and back again with only an occasional, *"Caw, caaaw."* A red-winged blackbird answered from the rushes fringing the pond and flew past in a swooping arc.

As he witnessed the song and dance of these feathered companions, he let go of his cares and felt satisfied as a kind of peace replaced them. Once again, nature had worked its magic—a major spiritual reconstruction on his soul. Satisfied, he turned toward the house while full-throated birdsong echoed an affirmation.

He paused at the backyard barrel to see if any bird food remained to reward his friends for their uplifting music and pleasant company. Under the seed sack he lifted from the barrel, he was startled to discover an unopened bag of flour. Ah, food for the birds . . . and food for him.

A rummage through the kitchen cupboard turned up enough ingredients for two fragrant loaves of yeasty bread. A few handfuls of assorted dried beans, a can of tomatoes and *presto:* Rhode Island chili with freshly baked bread! Plenty for him *and* his landlady. Perhaps things were not as bad as they'd seemed.

Just as the two sat down to dine, the postman delivered a parcel from a friend: jam-and-honey spread. Suddenly, the meal became even more interesting!

He gazed at the feast spread before him and the friend

seated beside him and marveled at the gratitude he felt within.

Sometimes, he decided, *life's richest gifts are found at the bottom of the barrel.*

Margaret Kirk

Secret Ingredients

I press "play" on the VCR and sit back to watch the ten-year-old video. On it was my kids' attempt to record my father's secret ingredients as he prepared our annual Christmas meat pies.

"Hi, Mom." I see myself looking out of the screen, gesturing for Lisa to aim the camera at her grandfather instead.

"Hi, Grandpa," she says next as the camera sweeps his direction.

My dad nods in acknowledgement while he pries open the lid of a spice can.

"Mom, what are you doing now?" The camera swings back to me.

"The hard part, as usual." I make a production of stirring the meat in a large pot. "Dad, don't strain yourself shaking that spice can," I tease over my shoulder.

We're making meat pies—my family's holiday tradition.

As an adolescent, I was not particularly close to my father. After driving a delivery truck and unloading heavy

packages all day to support our large family, he barely had energy left to talk to me, except to ask me to get him another beer from the fridge or go buy him a carton of cigarettes.

But one Christmas, he expressed a desire to make meat pies like his mother had. Although he could figure out the filling, he didn't have a clue about the crust. Then my junior high home ec teacher gave me a recipe for no-fail pastry.

Mustering my courage, I approached Dad and suggested we team up and experiment with the pies. Much to my delight, he agreed to give it a shot.

I began the pastry crust in the morning. Following the instructions precisely, I blended the dough while Dad sautéed the meat in a large pot—equal amounts of ground chuck and ground pork. He added onions and then debated on the spices.

They were the tricky part. Allspice, savory, sage, thyme, cloves, salt and pepper. He added them all on instinct, guessing at the amounts. The meat simmered and teased our noses.

Meanwhile, I successfully rolled out the crust and placed it in a greased and floured pie plate. I held the empty pie shell close to the pot while my father ladled in bubbling meat. When we judged it full enough, I positioned the top crust, crimped the edges with the tines of a fork, brushed it all with milk, and popped it into the oven. We put together several for dinner.

The aroma of baking pies was encouraging. By the time they were done, the whole family was salivating. But, would the meat pies taste as good as they smelled?

Dad placed a slice on each of our plates. The pastry flaked when our forks cut through it. Then the first taste: eyes closed, nostrils flared, smiles appeared and a unanimous "mmm . . . mm" resounded around the kitchen table.

"This is really good," Dad winked at me, "but I think the meat is the best part."

"Oh, really? I don't think so," I teased back. "The crust is delicious; the meat is a close second."

The bantering continued until we finally agreed that neither would be any good without the other. I glowed with pride. We had worked—side-by-side—to replicate the old family recipe, my dad and I.

That was the start of our Christmas tradition.

As he aged, it became more difficult for my dad to do his part. Some years we made as many as fifteen pies and stirring such a large pot of meat was not an easy task. Finally, I recruited my children, Brian and Lisa, as our kitchen assistants.

One year, Dad got pneumonia and never fully recovered. The Christmas after he died, I couldn't bear the thought of making meat pies. Besides, they wouldn't be the same without his secret seasonings. But Brian and Lisa insisted we continue the thirty-five-year-old holiday ritual.

Forcing my mind to the present, I focus again on the video, curious to see what he adds to the pot.

But Dad smiles now from the television screen while he scrapes the last of his savory meat into a pie shell. As I struggle to position the top crust on this final, skimpy pie, someone off-camera suggests it should be for Uncle Bruce, who's always first in line to get his.

"Here, let me spit on it." I wink. "I hope he's not watching this video." Everyone laughs and the screen goes white.

Silence.

It occurs to me that I hadn't noticed a single label on the spices Dad used in the video. Yet a huge grin sweeps across my face when I realize we'd captured the secret ingredients after all.

The secret wasn't in the seasonings. It was in the people. The teasing and joking. The laughing and loving. And I know it was the working together—side-by-side—that made our Christmas meat pies so special.

Jane Zaffino

Common Sense

Select a cozy corner of your home to create a holiday haven—far from post-office lines, crowded malls and office parties—by engaging your senses.

Sight: Display something that delights you—ice skates from your childhood, an heirloom Bible opened to the Christmas story or even a basket of sea glass collected during last summer's vacation.

Sound: Hang tinkling wind chimes to catch a furnace draft or play an instrumental holiday CD.

Smell: Light a seasonal candle—bayberry, pine or peppermint. Or select a fresh-from-the-oven scent like gingerbread, sugar cookie or pumpkin pie.

Taste: Treat yourself to a soothing, warm drink. Hot chocolate with marshmallows? Spiced cider? Herbal tea?

Touch: Layer the area with comfortable pillows, a soft throw, your favorite slippers—perhaps a few toys to entertain the cat.

Then set aside time each day to envelope yourself in this sanctuary of simplicity.

Love

Between the Lines

Sometime last year, tucked in the muscled folds of a metropolitan newspaper in Italy, a diminutive advertisement tiptoed out to compete with screaming headlines.

Elderly, retired schoolteacher seeks family willing to adopt grandfather. Will pay expenses.

Eighty-year-old Giorgio Angelozzi had packed himself and his seven cats into the wrinkles of a two-room flat, along with his modest book collection of dusty Greek dictionaries and classics written by noteworthy ancients like Pliny and Horace and Kant. From this cramped home on a dead-end road, he occasionally maneuvered the hilly paths to a local village. But, for the most part, his scholarly, retired life was quiet. Too quiet.

Widowed seven long, lonely years, Giorgio found himself counting the number of words he spoke aloud each day. And on those days when he had nothing to say—even to the padding cats—the count was zero. A zero as hollow as his life.

To his dismay, he discovered he wasn't done giving and needing love.

Hungering for human contact, Giorgio made a thoughtful decision and put into motion a unique plan: He put himself up for adoption. His humble appeal in the classifieds of an area newspaper immediately captured the attention of an entire nation.

Giorgio's plight tugged at Italy's heartstrings, made it sit up and take notice. Government officials and villagers, counselors and commoners, clerics and laymen—all jolted to the core by this plea for adoption—took an internal accounting. The result? An immediate surge of response that brought more than offers of lodging. It brought eager offers of friendship. Of family life. Of . . . love.

After all, Giorgio didn't advertise himself as a mere tenant. He didn't seek a position as a part-time professor nor a salaried tutor. Instead, Giorgio sought a family willing to adopt a *grandfather*, a family willing to accept him as part of itself.

At one time or another, each of us—like Giorgio—must face life's tough, emotion-wrenching moments. We might deal with the trials of rejection, bankruptcy, terminal illness, loneliness, unhappy partnerships or even death. Love is the universal answer to our difficulties.

If we are fortunate, we realize the power of love—that spark of the divine inherent in each of us—to smooth and soothe, to heal and restore. We search for it in our relationships; we invite it into our lives. We admire it in others; we cultivate it in ourselves.

We grasp for it with both hands and, if we are smart, we give it away with both, understanding that love, like music, is a melody that lingers in the heart long after the words have been sung. It is the grace that allows us to feel for each other, to put ourselves in our neighbors' places. We see with their eyes, hear with their ears and feel with their hearts. Better yet, we learn to view others through God's eyes.

Giorgio moved his seven cats and his worn library to the home of his new family. Undoubtedly, he also packed enough warmth and memories to flourish wherever he settled, valued by this new family that love alone created.

The lesson we might all share from this Italian love story? *L'amore é come il pane. Bisogna che si faccia di nuovo ogni giorno.* "Love is like bread. It needs to be made fresh every day."

And what better time than this Christmas season to share *your* loaf, to reach out in love and adopt others into the embrace of your family's circle?

Sweets for the Sweet

Every year, between Thanksgiving and December 26, something mystical happens to me. The festive foods of Thanksgiving dinner start the process. Then Christmas music, piped from radio and DIRECTTV for an entire month, trips my alarm to *shrill.* Recipe ideas, over a half-century of them, cork to the surface like soda fizz.

Each chorus of "Rockin' Around the Christmas Tree" and "I'll Be Home for Christmas" transports me deeper and deeper into a rhapsodic trance that has my husband, Lee, shaking his head, mumbling and slanting me knowing looks.

"What?" I snap, stirring candy.

"You're doing it again." He saunters past, sniffing the chocolate mixture.

"Why do you want to spoil Christmas for me?" I glare at his back. He just doesn't *get* it.

"I hate to see you work yourself to death," he says, munching spoils from my fudge heap.

"Hey, I *love* working myself to death."

At the same time, something deep inside concedes that I *do* actually go a little mad. I can't rest until I whip up thirty pounds of walnut fudge, fifteen pounds of Mounds candy, five gallons of Rice Krispies/Snickers balls (so the grandkids can, once a year, eat to their hearts' content), ten dozen peanut-butter balls, twenty pounds of butter-scotch fudge, and—although I *swear* each year I'll not do them again—I cannot resist making several batches of yummy chocolate-toffee bars.

"But why so *much*?" Lee snatches a couple of toffee bars and crams his mouth full. I roll my eyes at his duplicity.

"Tradition," I say.

And, dear Lord, on one level, it *is*. But, I ask myself, does tradition alone justify my annual cooking frenzy? I've done it since I was a teen practicing home ec class recipes. During ensuing years, I involved the children in the fun, building happy memories, packaging gifts of food for friends and family.

Now, with the kids raised, the activity has become, at times, tiresome. Yet the urge persists. Mystified, I wonder, *What is the core of this crazy compulsion?*

Later, I browse through some old family photos.

"Look, here's my Two-Mama," I tell Lee. "Remember how, after we married, we used to visit during Christmas? As far back as I can remember, she always had goodies of every description to feed us. I loved the way she would always . . ."

Tears spring to my eyes. I *miss* her. She and PaPa have been gone for many years. I remind Lee how my grand-parents' fragrant house welcomed and cheered me during childhood holidays, how their table sprouted delectable treats and how she always had plenty. Two-Mama made sure her loved ones never left her home hungry, even loading us down with carry-home bags.

That's it!

My Yuletide frenzy evokes memories of Two-Mama's gift to me. *That's* what motivates me! I never felt more loved than there, in her home, knowing in my child's mind that she'd prepared all this in honor of me. She celebrated me with all those goodies. That was her way of loving.

I smile at Lee. "I guess now it's my turn to celebrate my loved ones. It's my way of loving them." He squeezes my hand in understanding.

So, five weeks later, here I am: ten pounds heavier, crash-landed back to sanity. I'm also exhausted.

"Y'know," I admit to Lee, propping my swollen feet on the coffee table, "I'm getting older. I believe next year I'll skip the candy-making thing."

"That's a good idea, hon." He winks at me.

This time, I vow I'll remain staunch. Immovable. At least until Thanksgiving rolls around, and I hear those first strains, "I'll be ho-o-me for Christ-maaaas . . ."

Emily Sue Harvey

Nickled and Dimed

I was sitting at my desk involved in paperwork one sunny May afternoon when the door opened, and a young boy, about nine or ten, came into the store.

He walked confidently toward me and said he wanted to purchase a gift for his father. His serious countenance made it obvious: This was a mission of importance.

As we wound through the furniture division of Loy's Office Supplies, he expressed dismay at the cost of each chair and lamp. Finally, I suggested a desk-pad set. With eyes glowing, he thoughtfully chose a maroon faux leather unit with matching pencil cup, memo holder and letter opener. His joy nearly matched my own—the whole process ate two hours of my time—and we headed toward my desk to finalize the sale.

"Okay, I'll be in every week to pay on this for my dad," said young Michael Murphy.

"And you'll pick it up just before Father's Day?" I asked.

"Oh, no, ma'am. This is for Christmas."

My mouth gaped as wide as my eyes when he handed

me his first payment: a nickel and two dimes. But that day changed all of our lives at Loy's.

As the months passed, neither rain nor snow kept Michael away. Week after week, he arrived promptly at four o'clock every Friday to make his payment. His mother stood outside during each recorded transaction, and one day I asked to meet her.

From her, I learned that Michael's father was out of work. She took in laundry and ironing to eke out a living for the family of seven. I felt badly, but I respected their pride and refusal of help. But with the approach of winter, all of us at Loy's noticed Michael wore only a thin sweater, no matter how deep the snow. We concocted a story about a stray coat left at the store—that just happened to be his size. It worked.

One day Michael ran in to announce he had a job— bringing in the newspaper and sweeping the front steps for an old lady down the street every day after school. The ten cents she paid each week would bring him closer to his purchase.

As the holiday season drew near, I feared Michael would not have enough money to pay off the gift, but my boss advised me not to worry.

Two days before Christmas, a dejected Michael came into the store. He hadn't earned enough money to make his final payment.

"Could I please take the present for my dad so he'll have it for Christmas?" His eyes bored straight into my own. "I promise I'll be in after Christmas to finish paying it off."

Before I could answer, my boss looked up.

"Why, young man, there's a sale on desk sets today." He glanced at a paper in his hand. "I think it's only fair that you get the sale price, too."

That meant his dad's gift was paid for!

Michael raced outside to tell his mother. Amid teary hugs and broken thank-yous, we sent them on their way, with Michael clasping the precious, gift-wrapped present to his chest. All of us were proud of Michael's commitment to his project and his devotion to the dad he loved so much.

A few weeks after Christmas, a shabbily dressed man came into Loy's and limped directly to my desk.

"Are you the lady my son Michael talks about?" His voice was gruff and as oversized as the man himself.

When I nodded, Mr. Murphy paused. He cleared his throat.

"I've just come to thank you for all your help and patience. We don't have much," he picked at his worn glove, "and I still can't believe that youngster would do this for his old dad. I'm awful proud of him."

Rising from my chair, I walked around the desk to give him a hug. "We think Michael is pretty special, too. As we watched him pay off that desk set, it was clear he loves you very much."

Mr. Murphy smiled in agreement and walked away. But as he approached the door, his head swiveled my way and he blinked back the tears.

"And you know what? I don't even own a desk!"

Binkie Dussault

Fair Game

The real intent of our holiday trips to my wife's family in Oregon is for her to visit with her sisters and niece, along with shopping and cooking, of course. So I'm left twiddling my thumbs a lot, nobody to play with. Except my nephews Adam, Jimmy and Tyler.

A few years ago, I initiated an "Uncle and Nephews' Day" when we go out in force and spend time together doing something, somewhere. Bowling, skiing on Mt. Hood, whatever. Unbridled fun and freedom from parents with rules that only uncles and nephews share. Secrets and promises kept, love secured.

This time, I suggest a drive to the Coast Range west of Portland to an elk refuge called Jewell Meadows where hundreds of magnificent Roosevelt elk congregate.

"It's awesome," I assure my nephews. "Warm steam shoots from their black nostrils as they sound an eerie paean," I wax poetic. "We'll hear big bulls bugle their mating calls and see them proudly standing at attention as they oversee their harems."

The nephews say they're game.

On a cold, damp December morning, nephews and uncle—puffed in parkas—pile into an old sedan and head west in anticipation. The guys are loose again!

Now, Uncle hasn't been to Jewell Meadows in a couple of years maybe, but feels certain he knows the way.

Wrong.

Taking the well-remembered turnoff to the north and the I'm-sure-we-go-left-here crossroad, the beige Volvo wanders onto snowy mountain roads that become more and more unfamiliar.

The three nephews, ages twelve to fifteen, hurl taunts that are immediately challenged, which escalates into an exchange of witticisms and good-natured personal insults.

It's a guy thing.

It's how guys show love: taking potshots at each other, poking at each other's weaknesses and sensitivities. It's primitive preparation for the competitiveness they'll face as men in this still occasionally Neanderthal world of aggressive mentalities. Whether blue- or white-collar combat, it's all the same. This banter toughens them and keeps them tough, with an underlying, supportive subtext of love.

An uncle is a special being, both buddy and adult authority figure. More slack than dad, more unguarded camaraderie. An equal for a nephew—but an equal with acknowledged wisdom amid his playfulness.

An uncle is like a god, but pleasantly flawed and bemused by earthly existence. An uncle lets you in on the secret: Nobody really knows what life is all about, but don't worry about it. Be a good person and enjoy life to its fullest.

Heck, everyone's lost in the winter woods looking for elk and laughing their tails off over Uncle's ramblings. Ain't it great?

After two hours of wandering—with the required detours: roadside pit stops to pee, snowball fights in drifts with dog piles of nephews on top of Uncle, then pushing the car back onto the road from icy shoulders—Uncle stumbles onto the road to Jewell Meadows.

But today, the long-sought meadow—historically popu- lated with 400 to 500 regal animals against verdant green grass and bucolic woods beyond—is abo-so-lutely . . . *empty*.

Not an elk in sight.

"So, Uncle, where's the elk? We don't see any elk." Nephews are on Uncle's case.

Uncle's heart sinks; his male ego falters; his child lead- ership merit badge is at risk. Uncle's macho dissolves into nacho.

"I don't know," Uncle stammers. "They're *always* here, *hundreds* of them. This is weird. Maybe they're off in the tree line browsing. They do that sometimes. Let's get out of the car and walk up to the fence. Take the binoculars, too. They've got to be here somewhere."

All four guys zip up parkas, snug down wool caps, grab the binocs and creep to the fence.

Eyeing the tree line some three hundred yards across the meadow, they stare and stare. They begin to halluci- nate. First, individually, then en masse.

"I see one."

"Look over there, just past that big, funny-looking bush."

"THERE. See it? See, it's moving."

But no amount of conviction unearths an elk. It's cold;

snow is on the ground; they've crossed the continent for the Promised Land and there's no gold. No milk. No honey.

Nothin'.

Uncle rallies. "Oh, I get it."

Eyes hopeful, the three defeated nephews swivel their heads as one in his direction.

Uncle nods knowingly. "It's Christmas time, that's why."

"Huh? What's that got to do with it?" all three demand.

"Remember . . ." and, on the spot, Uncle begins a serenade. His voice floats over the entire meadow, a new twist on an old carol.

"No-o-elk, No-elk . . ."

The nephews are stunned. They actually lean away from Uncle, mouths agape, struck dumb, incredulous.

"No-o-elk, No-elk . . ."

They can't believe what they're hearing. Adam, the eldest, recovers first. "You brought us all the way out here to do THAT?"

In turn, the others arrive at the same conclusion: They've been had. Shagged. Deceived. Misled. Tricked.

"Aw, man."

"I can't believe it."

"Du-ude . . ."

They turn from the fence and toward Uncle. He's about to be a dead man. He knows it—and he can't wait.

The nephews attack full force, wrestle him down, pound on him, sit on him, jump on him and pelt him with snow. He resists not at all.

It's great. He earned it; he loves it. He loves *them.*

And they love him.

James Daigh

Nothin' Says Lovin' Like . . .

Christmas was coming, and I didn't have one ounce of spirit or energy. I couldn't even muster a half-hearted "ho-ho." I was a gray heap of sorrow, enmeshed in my own pity party.

I had taken a last walk with my closest friend that year and still grieved her passing. Neither of my away-from-home daughters would be able to get back for the holidays. My recently retired husband, grappling with his own identity, didn't or couldn't see that I was a mess. My joints ached; I felt old, looked old and was losing my grip on things that had always been so sure and steady in my life. I slogged through my days, unable to even recognize myself.

I mourned for the past when everything ran smoothly: The girls were growing; I was busy and involved in their lives; my husband was working. My grief had reached crisis proportions after our move across town a few months earlier. Even my neighbors had been replaced with strangers.

I tried walking the new neighborhood. I tried holiday shopping. I even saw a movie or two. But I felt like I had lost my way. Then the phone rang one afternoon.

"Isabel," a voice chirped. "It's Julie. Nicholas is wondering if you're planning your annual cookie-baking day. Are you?"

Ever since Nicholas was able to toddle across my kitchen in the old neighborhood, we'd had tea together and baked cookies. This year, his younger brother Zachary was old enough to join the activities.

"Oh Julie, I don't think . . ." I paused and mustered some false enthusiasm. "Of course I'm going to bake with Nicholas. And send Zachary along, too. It'll be great!"

I set the date and hung up the phone with a weight sitting in the bottom of my stomach like a wad of raw cookie dough. This was the last thing in the world I wanted—two little boys racing all over my house, my kitchen and my life. Still, it *would* be nice to carry on an old tradition.

Down the block lived another child, a quiet little thing, sometimes peeking out at me from behind a large ash tree in her front yard. One day I saw her sitting idly on the curb and, recognizing a kindred spirit, joined her.

"Hi. I'm Isabel. I moved in over there," I pointed, "and I'm lonesome because I don't know anybody. What's your name?"

"Kelsey," she answered. "I don't have anything to do."

"Hmm. Well, I've got just the thing," I heard myself saying. "Tomorrow my friends Nicholas and Zachary are coming to bake cookies. Would you like to come?"

Kelsey's mother eagerly brought her over the next morning. Standing on my doorstep were three grinning kids and two parents. I told the grown-ups that it would take about three hours, but I'd call when everybody was ready to go home.

And the four of us got started.

We measured.

We mixed.

We laughed when flour powdered our faces and hair.

The dough was over-rolled and over-handled, but it didn't seem to matter. Nor did anyone care when the cookie-cutter shapes were crooked or lopsided. And there were no tears shed over the burned sheet of Christmas trees that set off the smoke alarm. Instead, we discovered they made splendid Frisbees to bulls-eye the frozen bird-bath out back.

Amid singing and conversations both long and short, I hauled out the frosting: red and green pastry tubes that oozed both top and bottom. After a minilesson in rosette making, the three little ones practiced squeezing the sugar concoction onto the countertop. Did you know that red and green icing turns mouth, teeth and tongue an awful purple? Even my own!

Tiny fingers pressed raisin eyes and red cinnamon buttons onto gingerbread fronts. The kids ate two for every one they used. Colored sugar sprinkled the table, the Santa cookies and the floor.

Secrets were whispered, little hurts mended and problems solved while we downed three refills of beyond-sugary sugarplum tea in real china cups.

And—miracle of miracles—frosted holiday cookies, divided by lacy paper doilies, were all neatly packed in white boxes decorated with "Merry-Christmas-I-love-you" tags when the doorbell rang. *Six* hours later.

"I thought you came here to decorate cookies, not your-selves," Kelsey's mother teased. All three kids grinned back with purple teeth. I kept my own mouth closed.

"I miss you, Isabel." Nicholas grabbed me around the waist before he left. "The lady in your old house doesn't make us cookies or tea."

"Yeah," chimed in Zachary.

"One day," I smiled, holding Nick's rosy cheeks in both my hands, "you're going to grow up, and you won't want to bake Christmas cookies anymore. And I'll understand."

"Oh no, Isabel! I will never, never be too old for you. I love you."

"I love you, too," said Zachary.

"Me, too," whispered Kelsey.

And suddenly they were stuck to me like Velcro.

Christmas came. I invited all the old neighbors and a few of the new ones. My daughters phoned, bereft and homesick, and, of course, we all cried. I still missed my friend. And my husband didn't change at all. But the most important thing I learned that year was:

When life seems sorrowful—reach out.

Find children.

Bake cookies.

Isabel Bearman Bucher

Chords of Love

She lay prostrate on the wooden floor, unable to lift her head or move her body. Five minutes passed. Ten. Fifteen. All because she'd reached for a Christmas ornament and fallen out of her wheelchair.

What a day for John to be late, she thought, as her immovable position grew more and more uncomfortable.

The wedding photo on the table had tipped over with her. Out of the corner of her eye, she saw a beautiful bride and a handsome groom, each with Irish blue eyes and dark hair. Friends told her that raising three children hadn't aged either of them one bit.

John's car crunched in the snowy driveway. Her heart pounded as she heard him leap the stairs of their split-level home two at a time, eager to see his wife. Stunned to find her on the floor, John dropped to his knees—and wept with her.

Not out of sympathy. Peg's quips disarmed any of that maudlin stuff. Out of love—the deepest kind.

At that almost sacred moment, I intruded. "Oh I'm sorry," I said.

According to my custom as Peg's physical therapist, I had knocked and let myself in. Her husband dried his tears, scooped up her thin body, paralyzed from multiple sclerosis, and carried her to the bathroom. This was his habit every lunch hour.

"I'd do the same for you if things were reversed," Peg told him, her pluck restored.

"No you wouldn't. I'm too big for you," he said with a broad smile as he placed her back in her electric wheelchair, flipped on the Christmas tree lights and left for work.

"Do you hurt today after the fall?" I took off my hooded coat and red scarf.

"No, go ahead and do the routine," Peg said, then added, "I went to the counselor yesterday."

"How did that go?" I stretched her arm.

"Okay, until he asked, 'How's your intimate life?' I answered him, 'Fine, how's yours?' That quieted him right down."

No one tampered with this lady's love life or, for that matter, with her willingness to persevere. When therapy was over, she asked me to place a nativity set on her lap tray so she could arrange it. She knew her fingers were useless, but hey, why not give it a try? It was the holidays.

I shook my head with wonder.

Eager to show my love for this special couple, that very evening I gathered a group of carolers outside their family room window. I saw Peg seated in her wheelchair before the fireplace and John behind her like a tall, protective sentinel.

One, two, three. We struck the first chords, "Deck the halls with boughs of holly . . ." Trombone lifted, bells ringing, we sang a festive medley.

They invited us in for our grand finale, "We Wish You a Merry Christmas." The oven smelled of John's pumpkin bread. A little shy of strangers, they retreated to the back of the garland-strewn room.

When we strolled away, I glanced through the frosty window at Peg's forever smile. Her husband had resumed his attentive stance—her guardian, lover, friend for life. Oh, sure, Peg and John were pleased we had serenaded them. But their happiness came not from others. It came from an unbreakable cord of love, the kind that binds.

Once upon a time I had skimmed through a photographic album about couples. The artist prefaced his work with the words, "We two form a multitude." Surely, he must have known Peg and John.

Margaret Lang

Charlie's Coat

She'd been on a halfhearted hunt for some misplaced Christmas stockings when she found the coat—warm and soft, brown and dear—in the very back of her bedroom closet, hiding behind a big box of Glenn Miller albums. The sight of it shocked, surprised and saddened her. All three emotions gathered in one scary lump in the space between her throat and her permanently broken heart.

Why hadn't she found it before? Charlie had been gone a year to the day, and she'd been in that closet countless times. She'd pilfered through it like a teary-eyed madwoman looking for bits and pieces of the man she'd loved all of her life, things that were his, things he'd worn. Faded flannel shirts—his second skin from September through every April—broken-in Levi's with permanent white creases sharp enough to slice a loaf of homemade bread and his shoes.

Oh God, the shoes.

Empty shoes, just sitting there all alone. Except for the coat, they were the hardest things to look at. Reebok walkers, white on white, his old standbys. She'd bought them just two weeks before he passed away.

Where was the man who filled those shoes?

Not here. Not sitting with her on the side of the bed, not out in the woodshop, not at the corner take-out, not jawing at the fence with the neighbors, not dangling a grandkid on his knee, not here in this house.

Where he belonged.

Ginny made herself stand, take two small steps, and with eyes closed, reach to the back of the closet. There, she thought. She felt it. See? She could feel that coat and not go to pieces. But could she hold it, asked a small, inner voice. Could she smell it, look at it? And while she wondered, it hit her again . . . how did it get here, and where had it been for a whole, long year?

She'd told the kids she wanted it back. She didn't care which one of them had taken it. She knew it was out of love that they conspired to hide it away, like a piece of hurt she wouldn't have to see. She knew, she knew . . . out of sight, out of mind.

But they had insisted, all three of them, that they did not hide the coat, the chocolate brown barn coat she'd given him their first Christmas, 1962. The one he wore to work every day for the next twenty-five years, the one she'd teasingly threatened to toss away when the pockets wore off and the deep ribs became smooth and dull and the points on the collar curled up. The one he insisted on keeping long after it was presentable.

In less than a breath, she reached up now, on her toes, and tugged at the coat with all the loneliness and despair and gut-wrenching longing that was in her, and just as suddenly, with great care and respect and love, she pulled it to her small, shaking frame and slipped it on, one arm at a time, until she could double the breast, and then held on tight, and remembered.

"A bee-yoo-tee-ful lady I knew bought it for me," he'd said, "and I'm not about to give it up."

She still remembered the pain and the pride she'd felt when he'd said that, looking at her like she was the best thing he could ever hope to possess, and she'd understood. He most certainly had been the finest thing she had ever known.

And oh, that did it. That single, long-ago moment broke the dam. Just his quiet words, "It was the first time in my life, Ginny, that anyone ever loved me enough to buy me a new coat, a brand-new coat. Thank you for that, for loving me like that."

And after the horrible pangs of his sudden death, she'd searched for it everywhere. She'd torn the house up looking for it and hadn't been able to find it. But now here it was, one year later, wrapped all around her. The snow was falling, the Christmas bells were ringing, it was growing dark, and here it was.

Ginny pulled the coat tighter and bent her face to the collar. She breathed in and found the scent of pine woodchips, English Leather, good, strong coffee . . . and Charlie. She took another deep, deep breath from way, way down and every moment she'd ever shared with him flashed before her mind and her heart, and she snuggled even further into the warmth.

Oh, yes. She'd loved him that Christmas so long ago. And all the Christmases in between. And she loved him still, this Christmas, when there was nothing left of him except the memories.

And his old brown coat.

Robin Clephane Steward

Flashing Back

It wouldn't be Christmas without the memory of my dad taking the annual holiday photo. I carry a mental image of his hairline with the camera blocking his face and the unsnapped case dangling beneath it like the protective gear of a catcher's mask.

But nothing protected Dad from the hubbub of five kids on Christmas Day. The Christmas commotion clashed with his German temperament, driving him to create order out of the chaos.

So he created the ritual. None of us could eat dinner, or even touch our forks, before he took the holiday picture. His payoff was some peace, if only for a precious few minutes.

"I need quiet," he commanded, "or else it will take me even longer to set up."

We rolled our eyes—the only things we could move without disturbing the pose. The focus of his attention was a Zeiss Ikon Contaflex One, purchased when we were stationed in Europe. A manual 35 millimeter camera, it required endless calculations and adjustments before he dared click the shutter. I'm sure it was a dad just like him who inspired some kid to invent the Kodak Instamatic®!

For what seemed like hours leading up to the photo, he made us sit still in our assigned places around the table. He looked through the viewfinder every few seconds. He read—and reread—the instruction booklet. He peered through reading glasses to carefully manipulate the camera's settings.

And Mom offered us no sympathy.

"Be patient with your father," she advised. "Someday, when you're grown up, you'll thank him for doing this."

It turns out Mom was right.

Years after leaving home, I pawed through a box in her basement and discovered the Christmas pictures. I looked closely at each one and realized that, instinctively, Dad had almost replicated the poses each year. The changes were so minor that the photos resembled animation cells. I placed them in chronological order, earliest at the bottom, and began to flip through the years.

I notice how the images changed at the sides of the table where a highchair moved in and out of the frame like a ping-pong ball as each toddler grew out of it. Finally, Gretchen, Carolyn, Jan and I were all seated at the table. Seven frames later the high chair moved into place again with the family caboose, Bart. Our heights increased with the years and so did our hairstyles: from pixie, to beehive, to pageboy. We were always in Sunday dress, and Mom's clothes mirrored the decades.

But little changed at the head of the table.

With no evidence of him dashing to his own spot in front of the camera, Dad sported an every-hair-in-place military crew cut. He always wore a white shirt and a necktie that exactly matched his trousers. His left hand gripped an oversized fork impaling the turkey breast. His right hand held a knife poised to carve. It is a sign of the times when I see a white cord that stretched from a wall socket to Dad's new electric knife.

It's all there, captured year after year, as we held our places and our smiles, waiting for the Dad's diligently pre-set timer to click our pose.

My life story is told in those photographs, in all that is seen and unseen. And I smile, recalling the adage about what a picture is worth. Thank goodness Dad loved us enough to ignore our groans and snap them.

Kathryn Beisner

It's So Lover-ly

Adopt someone into *your* family this holiday season to shower with love by selecting from the following:

Open your home: Look at your circle of acquaintances with new eyes. Do you know a college student who can't travel home this Christmas? A co-worker with no relatives? New neighbors in the house next door? A recently widowed church member? Think of them as extended family—and invite them to share your holiday dinner.

Adopt a grandmother: Contact an area nursing center or retirement home and request the name of a lonely, aged resident. Make her your honorary grandmother. Visit, call and bring thoughtful gifts. Give freely of your time—and remember to continue this new relationship throughout the year.

Become an angel: Take advantage of opportunities during December to reach out to others. Contribute to the mall mitten tree, to a single parent through your civic club or to a homeless teenager through a local shelter. Fill their requests, slip in a luxury item or two, and do it with the same generosity of spirit you'd show your own children.

Kindness

Mounting Evidence

"If you were arrested for kindness," someone once asked, "would there be grounds to convict you?"

What an amazing concept, especially in a time when everyone is talking about it, but so few people seem to really be practicing it. Searching the Internet for the mere word brings a staggering 1,320,000 hits. Entire Web sites revolve around the topic. Countless essays expound complicated theories on the subject. Organizations like Compassionate Kids, Kindness Inc., Operation Kindness and the Human Kindness Foundation base their straightforward mission statements on it. Local, national and worldwide movements promote an entire revolution of it.

And with good reason.

These are hard times that try our souls. Hard times in the country, in the city, in the neighborhood, on the block. In all these places we find children wearing bruises and adults wearing hard faces. We find barren larders, drained pocketbooks and leaking hearts. We find wandering souls and aimless bodies. Withered minds and empty arms. The housebound and the homeless. Loneliness. Despair. Fear.

Suffering.

It may not be us personally, but the people are there.

Yet, underlying it all is mankind's eternal hope. Hope that

things will be better, people will be fixed, diseases cured, the poor made rich . . .

So for now we rely on human kindness, the healing balm for all that ails us. For it is by being kind, we have discovered, that suffering is eased and joy is spread.

Practicing the art of kindness makes life better for everyone—the giver and the receiver. Whether spontaneous or premeditated, uncomplicated or complex, kindness-in-action strikes a positive influence.

It's a simple word, with an equally simple definition.

Kind: of a friendly, generous or warmhearted nature.

Kindness: the quality—or state—of being kind.

So how difficult is it to adopt this virtue? To make it a natural quality in ourselves? To actually *become* kind, warmhearted beings?

A college professor once said, "Kindness is inherent in all of us. It is our inner urge to imitate the divine, to give of ourselves."

But even good intention doesn't necessarily beget kindness. Just ask Gladys.

A generous gift-giver, she thought of the holidays as an opportunity to share her modest wealth with friends and extended family. However, at ninety-three, she found shopping to be a monumental task. Instead, she decided to insert checks of equal value in everyone's Christmas cards.

In a rush to send them, Gladys kindly penned, "Buy your own present this year," then she put the cards in the mail.

It wasn't until after the holidays that she discovered all the checks—buried under papers on her desk!

Like Gladys's mislaid checks, kindness is sometimes buried in the rush of life. And isn't that a shame? Especially when it's a character trait so easy to claim, so easy to incorporate, moment by moment and day by day.

Look around. Miss Manners preaches it: Be polite. Oprah—along with countless others—encourages it: Commit "random acts of kindness." And the movie *Pay It Forward* spells it out: Kindness begets kindness.

It really *is* as simple as that.

Kindness is *niceness,* a common moral decency, or—plainly—doing what is right, what is polite. It doesn't falter in the face of religion, politics, gender or race. Kindness anticipates needs, creates value and substance, makes a difference—on a scale large or small, in random doses or in huge gulps. Kindness generates ripples without end. The more we offer, the more we will have to offer. Best of all, it's contagious—others pass it on.

Mother Teresa urged:

> *Spread love everywhere you go. First of all, in your own house . . . let no one ever come to you without leaving better and happier. Be the living expression of God's kindness: kindness in your face, kindness in your eyes, kindness in your smile, kindness in your warm greeting.*

Her message is clear. And simple. Those who follow it can shout in one voice, "The evidence is in. We're guilty as charged! Convict us all on grounds of kindness!"

Drawn to the Warmth

Factoring in the windchill, I knew the temperature was below zero. The bitter cold cut through my Californian sensibilities, as well as my enthusiasm as a tourist, so I ducked through the nearest door for warmth . . . and found myself in Washington, D.C.'s Union Station.

I settled onto one of the public benches with a steaming cup of coffee—waiting for feeling to return to my fingers and toes—and relaxed to engage in some serious people-watching.

Several tables of diners spilled out into the great hall from the upscale American Restaurant, and heavenly aromas tempted me to consider an early dinner. I observed a man seated nearby and, from the longing in his eyes, realized that he, too, noticed the tantalizing food. His gaunt body, wind-chapped hands and tattered clothes nearly shouted, "Homeless, homeless!"

How long has it been since he's eaten? I wondered.

Half expecting him to approach me for a handout, I almost welcomed such a plea. He never did. The longer

I took in the scene, the crueler his plight seemed. My head and heart waged a silent war, the one telling me to mind my own business, the other urging a trip to the food court on his behalf.

While my internal debate raged on, a well-dressed young couple approached him. "Excuse me, sir," the husband began. "My wife and I just finished eating, and our appetites weren't as big as we thought. We hate to waste good food. Can you help us out and put this to use?" He extended a large Styrofoam container.

"God bless you both. Merry Christmas," came the grateful reply.

Pleased, yet dismayed by my own lack of action, I continued to watch. The man scrutinized his newfound bounty, rearranged the soup crackers, inspected the club sandwich and stirred the salad dressing—obviously prolonging this miracle meal. Then, with a slow deliberateness, he lifted the soup lid and, cupping his hands around the steaming warm bowl, inhaled. At last, he unwrapped the plastic spoon, filled it to overflowing, lifted it toward his mouth and—with a suddenness that stunned me—stopped short.

I turned my head to follow his narrow-eyed gaze.

Entering the hall and shuffling in our direction was a new arrival. Hatless and gloveless, the elderly man was clad in lightweight pants, a threadbare jacket and open shoes. His hands were raw, and his face had a bluish tint. I wasn't alone in gasping aloud at this sad sight, but my needy neighbor was the only one doing anything about it.

Setting aside his meal, he leaped up and guided the elderly man to an adjacent seat. He took his icy hands and rubbed them briskly in his own. With a final tenderness, he draped his worn jacket over the older man's shoulders.

"Pop, my name's Jack," he said, "and one of God's angels brought me this meal. I just finished eating and hate to waste good food. Can you help me out?"

He placed the still-warm bowl of soup in the stranger's hands without waiting for an answer. But he got one.

"Sure, son, but only if you go halfway with me on that sandwich. It's too much for a man my age."

It wasn't easy making my way to the food court with tears blurring my vision, but I soon returned with large containers of coffee and a big assortment of pastries. "Excuse me, gentlemen, but . . ."

I left Union Station that day feeling warmer than I had ever thought possible.

Marion Smith

School of "Hire" Learning

I wrinkled my nose and sniffed the air as I closed the classroom windows; still, I couldn't identify the faint odor. But it was Friday afternoon, my first week of teaching, and—although already in love with my hardworking students—I was exhausted and ready to leave the building.

For the most part, my twenty-four fifth-graders were the children of seasonal agricultural workers on Long Island. Their parents were employed at the local duck farm, many on welfare. They lived in converted duck shacks, with outside privies, cold-water hand pumps and potbellied, wood-burning stoves.

So odors weren't that unusual.

However, by Monday morning the foul smell overpowered the hot room. Like a dog scenting its prey, I sniffed until I found it: a rotting sandwich in Jimmy Miller's desk, the bread smeared with rancid butter and the meat green. I rewrapped the sandwich, put it back in his desk and threw open all the windows before my students filed in.

At noon, the children got their lunch bags and fled to

the playground picnic table. I saw Jimmy unwrap his sandwich and pretend to eat. Making certain the kids didn't see, he wrapped it again, put it in his pocket and slipped it back into his desk when the class returned.

My stomach knotted in empathy over Jimmy's poverty . . . and his pride.

After a private discussion, another teacher and I "hired" Jimmy for classroom chores like cleaning the chalkboards. As payment, we treated Jimmy to lunch with us each day. We also encouraged him to study and provided him with after-school tutoring. Before long, Jimmy took pride in his special lunches and earned top grades in all his subjects. As word traveled through the faculty grapevine, Jimmy was "rehired" by each year's succeeding teacher.

After a time, however, I accepted another teaching position and moved away.

It was on a trip back eleven years later that my friend Chris asked if I remembered Jimmy. "He's attending college now and is home for Christmas break. When I mentioned that you were coming, he asked to see you. "

"Really? He was just a little shaver when I knew him."

"He's grown some since then." Chris tried to hide a smile. "Says he has a Christmas present for you."

"A gift? For me?"

Jimmy drove up a bit later, and I walked out to meet him. At 6'6" and pushing 280 pounds, he certainly was no longer a little shaver.

"Happy holidays." Jimmy stuck out an oversized paw. "I hear you got your doctorate. Congratulations! Do you mind if I call you Doc?"

"It's all right with me, Jimmy." I tilted my head and

looked up the full length of him. "What have you been doing?"

"Well, I got a four-year football scholarship, and I've made the dean's list every semester. I graduate in June."

"Great work. I bet you've signed a pro contract already. Big bucks, you know."

"Yeah, I've had a few offers, but I'm not goin' into the pros."

"No kidding. Why not, Jimmy?"

"I have other plans."

"Oh?"

"I finished my student teaching last week, Doc." He smiled when I registered surprise. "I've decided to be a teacher—just like you." For a quiet moment, Jimmy gazed over my shoulder . . . and into the past. "I know you fellas invented those classroom jobs for me." He cleared his throat. "You helped me keep my dignity, and I've never forgotten."

I felt a lump in my own throat as Jimmy looked me full in the face.

"When teachers really care, students know it," Jimmy said. "That's why I want to teach. I want to be there for my students the way you were there for me."

What a Christmas gift, I thought. And, a little teary eyed, we shook hands.

No longer teacher and pupil, we were now two men with the same hopes—and the same goals.

Edmund W. Ostrander

Surprise Santa

A few days before Christmas, a devout Christian couple held the hands of their young son and walked briskly to their nearby church. But the boy pulled back a bit, slowed and came to an abrupt halt.

"Santa," he whispered. "Santa!"

The four-year-old broke free of his parents' grasp and ran toward an elderly gentleman with a long, flowing white beard.

Tugging on the stranger's coattail, the youngster begged, "Santa, will you bring me a teddy bear for Christmas?"

Embarrassed, the couple started to apologize, but the man merely waved them aside. Instead, he patted their son on the head, nodded once, winked wryly at the youngster and—without a word—went on his way.

On Christmas morning, a knock interrupted the family's festivities. In the doorway stood the old man holding out a large bear with a plaid bow around its neck.

"I didn't want the little fellow to be disappointed on his

holiday," he explained with an awkward grimace and turned to leave.

Uncomfortable and stunned, the parents could only stutter a weak, "Uh, th-thanks. And M-merry Christmas to you . . . Rabbi."

Henry Boye

In the Bag

As I step from the damp winter chill into the warmth of Carmen's living room, her cocker spaniel announces my visit with high-pitched barking.

"I'm in here," Carmen yells.

I pass the tabletop Christmas tree and find Carmen sitting in her wheelchair beside dozens of white paper bags standing at attention on the dining room table.

"Did you bring the goods?" she asks.

I nod, offering her thirty packets of Famous Amos cookies. Carmen smiles as I drop a package inside each sack. On Christmas Eve, Carmen delivers them to the thirty residents of Shalom House, a homeless shelter in Kansas City, Kansas, where her friend Mary Kay lives and works. I've heard about the bags for months and wanted to be a part of the fifteen-year tradition.

My understanding of homelessness is the guy on the freeway ramp carrying a cardboard sign asking for work or the men lying underneath bundles of blankets on the streets of Manhattan. Somehow, the packages of cookies

seem too small an offering for men who need so much.

Seventy-five-year-old Carmen fastidiously prepares the Christmas gifts like a doyenne tending to a queen. A shiny red Christmas card, embossed with a picture of gift-bearing wise men, is neatly taped to each bag. "May the Peace of Christ Be with You" is written across the top.

Carmen's cheery disposition and sense of purpose belie a myriad of health problems. Besides diabetes and congestive heart failure, neuropathy has destroyed the feeling in her swollen fingertips. It takes her a long time to move a pen or tear off a piece of tape.

"Look at all the stuff in here," I exclaim, noting that each bag already contains a razor, deodorant, Cheez-Its, Chex mix and other items buried on the bottom.

"There'll be more." Carmen proudly rattles off the names of friends yet to bring goodies.

The tradition began with Christmas cards containing a few crisp dollar bills. Over the years, she added shampoo, a pair of socks, a snack. Regardless of her meager Social Security check, she managed to increase the gifts each year.

Friends started to offer contributions. How about candy? A pair of gloves? The project evolved into a group effort involving dozens, each contributing thirty identical items.

"This year's bags are worth seventy dollars each." Carmen bobs her head in delight. "And they're stuffed so full that next Christmas I'll need even bigger ones!"

I wonder about the men at Shalom House and decide to visit the shelter after Christmas. It sits at the end of an empty lot, as abandoned as a beat-up toy. The inside is clean and homey, but unexpectedly quiet this time of morning; the men left early, hoping to find work.

But Carmen's friend, diminutive Mary Kay, is here. Resident mother and grandmother of Shalom House, she tends its day-to-day operations with stoic perseverance—as she has for seventeen years now.

"By the time they arrive here, the men have no place left to go," she says. "Shalom House represents hope—clean clothes, a hot meal, a bed and a family atmosphere. At least for a few days."

When I admire the well-adorned Christmas tree in the corner of the dining room, Mary Kay invites me on a tour.

The back room is lined with fifteen metal-framed bunk beds. A stuffed panda swings from a red ribbon over bunk #14. Shirts hang from the rafters because there is no room for dressers or lockers. A large closet is full of clean shirts, pants, underwear and socks.

"Most of the men arrive with just the clothes on their backs," she explains.

"What about Carmen's goodie bags?" I ask.

"Those sacks are the only present many of the men receive." Mary Kay points to a bunk bed, and I recognize the unmistakable evidence of Carmen's trademark taped above it: a shiny red Christmas card embossed with the picture of gift-bearing wise men.

"And do the men enjoy the gifts?" I wonder, still worried that it's too little, too . . . insignificant.

But Mary Kay rolls her eyes. "They love them. Why, the men immediately sit on their bunks, pour out the contents and start bartering. They get as excited as little boys trading baseball cards!"

Back in my car, I sit for a minute and start brain-storming about what I can contribute to Carmen's project next year. Umbrellas would be nice. Woolly stocking caps could be good. Or maybe some hand warmers?

Sheila Myers

Stroke by Stroke

I pushed through the crowd huddled in winter coats. There lay Blackie in the snowy street. I fell at my collie's feet and spread my arms around her as if to protect her from further injury. Not a car stirred that cold Sunday morning—nothing moved at all except her soft tricolor fur and my tears.

"Why don't they come?" I looked at the sad faces above me. "Why don't they hurry?" I was sure *they* would save her life . . . unfortunately there was nothing left to save.

My parents led me away, while, hand stretched back to my beloved pet, I called out to her for the last time, "Blackie, oh, Blackie."

Christmas joy extinguished as fast as the hit-and-run vehicle had skidded along the icy road. Tinsel on the tree lost its sparkle, stockings by the fireplace their promise, red and green chocolate kisses their sweetness. Without a collie curled up on the Oriental rug, gray became the holiday color.

Mom lost interest in her baking. My cousins no longer

pinned sequins on Styrofoam balls. My brother abandoned his ice skates. Worst of all, the carols on the stereo could not be heard above my relentless wail. The crying jag took on a life all its own. Even Dad's lap, usually the solution for all problems, held no answers at this time.

Until Grandfather got involved. "Can't someone stop that noise?"

Startled, I held my breath . . . not certain it was safe to sob anymore.

My Aunt Veramina's gentle words softened the atmosphere. "Come with me to your room, Margaret, so I can brush your hair."

My hand in hers, we followed the garland-wrapped banister up to the second floor of the big colonial house. She sat me down in a pink frilly chair and took my brush from the grooming set on the dresser top.

"Now, doesn't that feel better?" she asked as she loosened my long braids and with her competent hands, pulled the bristle brush through my thick auburn tresses.

The spasms of crying relaxed. A sniffle sputtered out. A whimper crept away. Finally, I filled my grief-weary lungs with one long restorative breath.

Under my aunt's soothing strokes of kindness, my head tilted back and forth. The rhythm, much like that of a rocking chair, changed the sadness of the day into the peace of the moment.

Sometime later, my braids and I bounced down the stairs. At my appearance in the living room, I heard a combined breath drawn. I leaned over the box of ornaments and, by coincidence, chose the large glass teardrop. This tear wasn't sad; it was merry, very merry—shocking pink with gold embroidered trim. When I hung it on the fragrant spruce, I felt a combined sigh of relief around me.

"Here," said Grandfather, as he handed me his peace offering of fresh pecans. With aged fingers around a silver nutcracker and pick, he had labored to extract the meat of six unbroken pieces for his granddaughter.

"Thanks, they're my favorite." I popped one into my mouth.

It seemed like someone suddenly flipped a power switch. The stereo hummed "Winter Wonderland." Sequins whizzed onto Styrofoam balls, powdered sugar onto cookies. And my brother zoomed toward the door, skates over his shoulder, "Anyone wanna join me at the park?"

Funny how on that tragic day, all the season's colorful trimmings and trappings combined had not been able to restore Christmas joy like one plain bristle brush in my aunt's hands. To be sure, I never forgot Blackie. But within a few days, a new collie dog had curled up beside me on the Oriental rug.

Margaret Lang

A Slice of Life

Jean heaved another world-weary sigh. Tucking a strand of shiny black hair behind her ear, she frowned at the teetering tower of Christmas cards waiting to be signed. What was the point? How could she sign only one name? That was half a couple, not a whole.

The legal separation from Don left her feeling vacant and incomplete. Maybe she could skip the cards this year. And the holiday decorating. Truthfully, even a tree felt like more than she could manage. She had cancelled out of the caroling party and the church nativity pageant. After all, Christmas was supposed to be shared, and she had no one to share it with.

The doorbell's insistent ring startled her. Padding across the floor in her thick socks, Jean cracked the door open against the frigid December night. She peered into empty darkness. Instead of a friendly face—something she could use about now—she found only a jaunty green gift bag perched on the porch railing. From whom, she wondered, and why?

Under the bright kitchen light, she pulled out handfuls of shredded gold tinsel, feeling for a gift. Instead, her fingers plucked an envelope from the bottom. Tucked inside was a typed letter. No, it was a . . . story?

The little boy was new to the overpopulated orphanage, and Christmas was drawing near, Jean read. Caught up in the tale, she settled into a kitchen chair.

> *From the other children, he heard tales of a wondrous tree to appear in the hall on Christmas Eve. Of scores of candles that would light its branches. Of the mysterious benefactor who made it possible each year.*
>
> *The little boy's eyes opened wide at the mere thought. The only Christmas trees he'd seen were through the fogged windows of other people's homes. There was even more, the children insisted. More? Oh, yes! Instead of the orphanage's regular fare of gruel, they would be served fragrant stew and crusty hot bread that special night.*
>
> *Last and best of all, the little boy learned, each of them would receive a holiday treat. He would join the line of children to get his very own . . .*

Jean turned the page. Instead of a continuation, she was startled to read: "Everyone needs to celebrate Christmas, wouldn't you agree? Watch for Part II." She refolded the paper while a faint smile teased the corner of her mouth.

The next evening, Jean rushed home from work. If she hurried there was probably enough time to decorate the mantle. She pulled out the box of garland but dropped it to race for the door when the bell rang. This time, she opened a red bag.

. . . to get his very own orange, Jean read. An orange? That's a treat?

> *An orange! Of his very own? Yes, the others assured him. One for each child. The boy closed his eyes against the wonder of it all. A tree. Candles. A filling meal. And—last and best of all—an orange of his very own.*
>
> *He knew the smell, tangy sweet, but only the smell. He'd sniffed them at the merchant's stall in the market-place. Once he'd even dared to rub a single finger over the brilliant, pocked skin. He fancied for days that his hand still smelled of orange. But taste one, eat one?*

The story ended abruptly, yet Jean didn't mind. She knew more would follow.

The next evening, her pile of unaddressed Christmas cards was shrinking when the doorbell rang. Jean wasn't disappointed. However, the embossed gold bag was heavier than the others had been. She tore into the envelope resting on top of the tissue paper.

> *Christmas Eve was all—and more—than the children had promised. The piney scent of fir competed with the aroma of lamb stew and homey yeast bread. Scores of candles diffused the room with golden haloes. The timid boy, at the very back of the line, watched in amazement as each child in turn eagerly claimed an orange and politely said, "Thank you."*
>
> *The line moved quickly, and he found himself in front of the towering tree and the equally imposing headmaster. "Too bad, young man, too bad. The head count was in before you arrived. It seems there are no*

more oranges. Next year. Yes, next year you will receive an orange." Brokenhearted, the empty-handed orphan raced up the stairs to bury both his face and his tears beneath his pillow.

Wait! This wasn't how she wanted the story to go. Jean felt the boy's pain, his aloneness.

The boy felt a gentle tap on his back. He tried to still his sobs. The tap was more insistent until, at last, he pulled his head from under the pillow. He smelled it before he saw it. A cloth napkin rested on the mattress. Tucked inside was a peeled orange, tangy sweet. It was made of segments saved—last and best of all—from the others. A slice donated from each of his new friends. Together the pieces made one whole, complete fruit.

An orange of his very own.

Jean swiped at the tears trickling down her cheeks. From the bottom of the gift bag she pulled out an orange— a foil-covered, chocolate orange—already separated into segments. And, for the first time in weeks, she smiled. Really smiled.

She set about making copies of the story, segmenting and wrapping individual slices of the chocolate orange. After all, she had visits to make. There was Mrs. Potter across the street, spending her first Christmas alone in fifty-eight years. There was Melanie down the block, facing her second round of radiation. Her running partner, Jan, single-parenting a difficult teen. Lonely Mr. Bradford losing his eyesight, and Sue, sole caregiver to an aging mother . . .

Perhaps, just perhaps, a piece from her might help make one whole.

Carol McAdoo Rehme

Sealed with a Kiss

Christmas is a wonderful time to share a favorite treat with a friend. Whip this up in triple batches and give them with a smile.

Kiss Kringles

¾ cup sugar
2 sticks softened butter
2 cups sifted flour

1 cup finely chopped pecans
8-ounce bag of chocolate candy kisses
powdered sugar for dusting

Cream together sugar and butter until smooth. Stir in flour; fold in pecans. Seal dough in plastic wrap and chill at least 30 minutes.

Remove foil from chocolate kisses. Completely cover each chocolate with enough dough to make a 1-inch ball. Place on ungreased cookie sheet and bake for about 12 minutes at 350°, until lightly firm.

Sift powdered sugar over tops while still warm. Makes 2½ dozen cookies.

Be extra kind: Package your cookies in decorator tins, on holiday trays, or in napkin-lined sewing baskets, small ice buckets, or cheery pottery bowls.

Gratitude

Steeped in Gratitude

You can make it quick: Plug in a single-serve, electric hot pot and dip a tissued teabag.

You can make it simple: Zap a stoneware mug of prebrewed in the microwave.

You can make it on-the-run: Propel your car into the nearest drive-through, place a quick order and pay at the window.

To get a cup of tea, you can do any of those things, and you probably have. But at what cost? Perhaps you're forfeiting a pleasure in the act itself.

Taking time to *plan* a proper cup of tea allows you to *pause* in the routine of daily life, to elevate yourself to a higher plane. Pull out a favored teakettle—well-worn and coppered, or plump and patinaed, maybe full-bellied and Dumbo-eared—and fill it with freshly drawn water. Wait for it to whistle.

And while you're waiting, attend to the details.

You might discover that *preparing* the tea tray brings its own peculiar *pleasure*. Gather those special items guaranteed to please: a whimsical cloth napkin, your grandmother's chipped, bone-china teapot, a quaintly mismatched cup and saucer, and a delicate silver spoon. Add your personal selection of sugar cubes, clovered honey, heavy cream or serrated lemon slices.

Then select your favorite flavor of loose tea. What will it be today? Traditional oolong, Ceylon or sage? Exotic jasmine, lingonberry or licorice? Or what about something Christmasy, maybe cinnamon-apple, peppermint or orange-tangerine?

And keep an ear cocked toward the kettle. First, you'll hear humming and hissing. Next, a full-throated gurgling, just before the kettle bursts into full song, whistling for your attention.

Serve your tea with the *ceremony* it deserves. Swill a bit of boiling water in Grandma's teapot, empty it out and add those flavor-filled leaves. Flood with burbling water. Cover. Simmer. Steep. Let the fragrant tendrils of steam seep from the spout to tempt and tickle your senses. Inhale, deeply.

Mind-mellowing, muscle-melting . . .

And when you've waited as long as you can, pour yourself a cup. Right to the brim.

Swizzle the lemon or dollop the cream.

Drizzle some honey or swirl a sugar cube. One lump? Two?

Now allow yourself the *serenity* to *savor* the full-bodied drink. Position your face to catch the last rays of the winter sun. Or prop your toes in front of a toasty fire. Puff away the steam . . . and take a test sip. Then another. And another. *Ahhhhhhhh.* Let its warmth seep through your limbs, thaw your tummy and soothe your soul.

A home-brewed cup of tea. Simple and satisfying. Perhaps all the more so because of the thought, the ritual and the repetition that created the experience itself.

Like brewing tea, gratitude is an art to be practiced, a virtue worth perfecting.

When was the last time you considered life's abundance? Felt appreciation for the small things? December's first snowfall, a thick comforter on a winter night, an empty bus seat when you're loaded with holiday packages. Or counted your larger blessings? A secure job, well-behaved teenagers and forgiveness from a mate.

Next, think about those who have touched your life. Has someone soothed an ache? Filled a void? Maybe you've been the recipient of a kind deed or an act of compassion. When you were torn, did someone mend you? When you were down, did someone lift you up? When you were tired, did someone carry you?

And, above all, did you remember to express your gratitude?

It's never too late to show your appreciation to others.

You *could* make it quick, simple, on-the-run. Or you can indulge in the full-bodied experience of expressing gratitude until the repetition itself becomes a ritual as natural and rhythmic as brewing tea.

Pause and plan a way to do it: How can you best acknowledge a thoughtful favor? What can you do to instill delight?

Take pleasure in the preparation: Give of yourself, your time, your emotions, your energy. Never rush an act of appreciation. Enjoy the process.

Serve it with a bit of ceremony: Use your best stationery and a fine-tipped pen, or pick the tightest buds from your prized rosebush.

By elevating gratitude to a virtue, you might discover your own heart warms in the process. So brew a satisfying cup of appreciation and fully *savor the serenity* . . . sip by tiny sip.

St. Nick's Note

As the weatherman promised, the temperature climbs to ninety-eight by midafternoon. I waste no time retrieving the mail from our box.

"Whew! The humidity must be 102." I collapse into a kitchen chair.

"You know it!" My husband agrees. He sits with both hands wrapped around a large glass of iced tea, still sweating after mowing the lawn.

"It's only July. Aren't you rushing the season a bit, Santa?" I tease.

"Are you referring to my red nose and cheeks?" He wiggles his bushy eyebrows. "Just getting a headstart on Christmas this year."

My jolly old St. Nick delights hundreds of children—of all ages—each December. Whether he's appearing at schools or in parades, he spreads his special Santa brand of love and kindness.

"Anything important?" He points at the mail on the table.

Fanning the pile, I hand him a farming magazine, a

soil-and-water conservation newsletter and this month's electric bill. Toward the bottom of the stack, I pause to inspect a small white envelope.

"You're not going to believe this." I turn the letter toward Alan. "It's addressed to Santa Claus."

"Well, maybe I'm not so early after all," he chuckles. But instead of a wish list, he pulls out a hand-decorated card. "Thank You" is scrawled across the front. A trace of moisture washes his eyes.

"Remember these little guys, Mrs. Claus?" He hands me the card.

Oh, yes, I remember.

Each year I help Santa make "special deliveries"—for organizations, church groups or even concerned individuals—to single-parent families, the newly widowed, recently divorced, unemployed or those whose income barely covers essentials. These anonymous deliveries from Santa mean more than gifts under their trees or dinner on their tables: These deliveries express love and concern.

And this card comes from one of those single parents.

A month before last Christmas, this young mother found herself single and the sole provider for her seven-year-old twins. When she'd escaped her abusive situation, she was forced to leave behind most personal items, including her sons' bikes. According to a caring counselor at the "safe house," the distressed woman dreaded explaining to her sons that Santa couldn't bring new bikes this year. She'd accepted all the help she felt she was entitled to and wouldn't ask for more. Besides, bikes were a luxury.

Her friends didn't agree.

Because of those friends, Santa and Mrs. Claus delivered quite a load of groceries, gaily wrapped presents—and two new bikes to the grateful mother. Identical blue-eyed, freckle-nosed faces burst into jack-o'lantern smiles a mile wide as they peeked around her skirt.

"Oh, my goodness . . . we can't . . . who are you?" she stammered.

"Santa, of course! And this is Mrs. Claus," my husband boomed with a wink at the boys. "You made a very special list this year, and we wanted to deliver these early."

Santa's parting, "Ho, ho, ho," still echoed on the porch when a small, excited voice reached us, "Mama, I told you Santa would find us, even if we have to hide from Daddy."

Opening the card that jolted my memory, I read aloud to Santa. "It took me seven long months to discover how to reach you. I was so surprised that morning you came, I'm not sure I remembered to thank you. You helped the healing process begin and gave us back faith and hope."

Twin smiley faces followed the mother's signature at the bottom.

They were identical to our own.

Pamela Bumpus

Mother to Mother

I sit in the audience with the other parents, beaming at our children filing into their seats. My little ones' black hair and sienna skin make exclamation points among the other, pastel angels forming the pageant choir.

The chorister raises her arm, and the pianist comes in with the downbeat. So do some of the kids—a bit early. In cherubic fervor, their words spill out, "I am a child of God . . ."

Oh, how I wish both of you could see this. They're perfect. Just perfect.

I often send this silent message to my children's birth mothers. I long to comfort and reassure them, to share with them the unspeakable joy their babies have brought into my life. I long to tell them their precious ones are beautiful and bright, healthy and strong.

". . . and he has sent me here . . ." I can almost distinguish Shyloh's sweet voice in the choir.

Just the other day, she asked, "Mommy, why is my hair black? Yours isn't."

The answer came easily to me. "To make you look beautiful, Shyloh, just like your mother in China." And typically Tiggerlike, she bounced away, grinning in satisfaction.

I hope you find peace in your decision to share this happy girl with me.

". . . has given me an earthly home, with parents kind and dear . . ." I catch the eye of my Samoan daughter, Whitney, whose hair is a shining cape flung across her shoulders and whose voice rings loudest of all the angels. She's singing with all her young heart.

She's adjusting, Mama. I grin through my burning eyes. *Your daughter's finally joining in. So is little Luke.*

My grateful tears plop down to bless the slumbering head of Whitney's contented baby brother, asleep on my lap.

What sacrifices these women made for their children, their difficult choices possible only because their powerful mother-love transcended all else. And what joy their decisions continue to bring into my life.

Whoever you are, wherever you are and whatever your circumstances, I hope your intuition calms you and tells you all is well.

Mother to mother, I wish I could wrap my arms around them this holiday season—those selfless birth moms— and assure them of my appreciation for these beautiful children of ours. More than anything, I wish I knew *how* to express the gratitude in my heart.

". . . I am a child of God, and so my needs are great . . ." Their angelic voices supplicate and saturate the auditorium and reach into the depths of my consciousness.

And—with sudden, deep conviction—I *do* know how, the only way that makes sense: I'll continue to love and cherish their little ones with all my being.

That will be thanks enough.

Annette Seaver

Chilly Today, Hot Tamale

"It's my own fault." Carl Fenter tugged his jacket closer against the abnormal bite of cold morning wind. "The rest of the family is home, where it's warm."

Just another one of his brilliant ideas—a big tamale feast after tonight's Christmas Eve service at church—and look where it landed him: waiting in a line fifty people deep.

Who would've guessed that every tamale shop in the city would be sold out the day before Christmas? But they were, as Carl knew. He'd been driving all over El Paso that morning. Determined to bring home the tamales, Carl tried one last *tienda,* an old favorite out in Canutillo.

When he arrived, a fresh batch was due off the steamer in forty-five minutes. Taking his place at the end of the snaking line of tamale-seekers, he watched the woman in front of him remove her jacket to drape around her shivering youngster. It wasn't long before she, too, shuddered in the chilly wind. After only a moment's hesitation, Carl shed his own jacket and offered it to the grateful mother.

Together, they cheered when the line crept forward at last, and smiling people exited the shop toting steamy bags. Finally, Carl got inside the door and inched his way closer to the counter, the woman now first in line.

"Sorry folks," the clerk announced, "that's the last of the tamales."

"No way!" Carl groaned with everyone else lined up behind him.

"But," stressed the man at the counter, "we'll have a final batch ready in, oh, about two hours."

Defeated, Carl backed away, but the young mother grabbed his arm.

"You're leaving?"

"I have to," Carl glanced at his watch. "I promised to put up luminarias at my church."

"I'll get your order of tamales and bring them to your house."

Carl's brow furrowed. "I couldn't ask you to do that."

"But it's the least I can do. You lent me your coat." Her smile overrode his objections. "Just give me your address." She and her little girl settled in for the long wait.

And at exactly noon on Christmas Eve, they delivered four dozen fragrant tamales—along with Carl's brown jacket—to his home.

Ellen Fenter
Submitted by Pat Phillips

A Piece of Themselves

Some see a group of women, twenty-three strong. Others see a group of twenty-three strong women. Everyone sees that their fingers are flying nearly as fast as their mouths.

Going to Pieces, the quilting guild at the Fort Drum, New York, army base, is at it again: their monthly sewing spree. It's a time each woman anticipates. A time to share patterns and platitudes. A time to trade ideas and intimacies. A time to join quilt blocks—and lives.

With many of their husbands deployed to the Middle East, the women seek relief in this regular gathering. Finding strength in numbers, they learn to emphasize life over loss, joy over loneliness and victory over defeat. In part, they achieve this closeness by telling stories— mostly about their children. They laugh over the latest toddler's antics, cringe over an adolescent's angst, roll their eyes over an update on teen fads and fashion. And the telling and sharing bind them into a sort of extended military family.

Even while war's dark cloud hovers over them, they

choose to meet and mingle—especially with the holidays creeping nearer.

But tonight's mood is somber.

Something is obviously absent: There are no Christmas patterns in sight. No button-eyed snowmen, beaded holly or smiling nutcracker appliqués in hoops. No splashes of seasonal snowflakes, gingerbread men or angel prints on tables.

There's no casual chatter about old favorites like Log Cabin, Irish Chair or Tumbling Blocks. Neither do any of the women introduce new patterns, show a quilt they've recently completed or suggest working on a sampler.

Tonight a reverence blankets the room. Rather than creating individual blocks to join, they know this particular quilt requires more—a personal piece of each of them to make the whole. The project they've chosen echoes that faraway place always so near in their minds: Iraq.

The pieces they cut with such precision come from a young man's clothes. His desert-sand camouflage—fatigues and battle dress uniforms that will never be worn again, never be needed again. The template they pick is Lover's Knot—the pattern they see as most symbolic of the quilt's purpose, as well as their own feelings. The pieces will fit together like a complex jigsaw puzzle.

And the women wish they could as easily fit together the fragments of their compassion, their unspoken grief, their empathetic heartbreak.

Each snip and stitch is done with the knowledge that this quilt will go to one of their own. The family of the oh-too-young soldier who paid the ultimate sacrifice for his country.

When memories dim—until there is nothing more than a feeling, a taste, a smell to remind him of the Daddy he'll never know—it will wrap a lonely child.

When night presses in—to remind her of the husband whose death left a jagged hole in the fabric of her life—it will swaddle a sobbing widow.

With this purpose in mind, these stoic women hold in tears of their own to cut and piece, quilt and bind. And, when their work is completed, they will bestow the quilt with love rather than pomp . . . with gratitude rather than ceremony.

Why?

Because these sorrowful sisters, above all others, understand the sacrifice involved, and this is how they choose to express their appreciation.

Carol McAdoo Rehme

Angels and Angst

Another dull church meeting. I muffled my third yawn. The old geezer was *still* droning on about church involvement. Same-old same-old. I was taking notes, substituting for my mom, the group secretary. But I had other things to do. Important, sixteen-year-old stuff. I doodled on the edges of the pad.

Deep in daydreams, I nearly missed the good-lookin' guy who walked in late and sat across from me. Tucking a wisp of hair behind my ear, I straightened in my chair and cocked a suddenly interested, furrowed brow toward Gramps, but sneaked a look from the corner of my eye when Mr. Cute raised his hand and took the floor.

I flashed him my most intelligent smile.

"I think more young people should be teaching in our Sunday schools," he was saying. "Don't you?"

I nodded wholeheartedly.

He continued, "It would be a good way for teens to feel like they're part of the church. All we'd need are volunteers."

Suddenly, with no direct input from me, mine was the

first hand to shoot into the air. I hoped he noticed. A second-grade Sunday school class was assigned to me. On the spot.

Oops.

For endless months of Sundays, I forfeited sleeping late to serve my "term" with a rambunctious bunch of seven-year-olds. *Term,* I decided, was synonymous with *serving a sentence.*

Skimping lesson preparation, I taught *my* way. I marched them around the room tooting pretend trumpets until the walls of Jericho collapsed—thankfully, just before I did. I awarded tiny gold stars for memorized Bible verses. I celebrated birthdays by counting out a penny per year to give to the poor. But, mostly, I got headaches from their unbridled enthusiasm and off-key renditions of "Jesus Loves Me."

The weeks plodded on, and so did I.

"Miss Whitley," the minister asked, "would you direct the Christmas program this year?"

I would, I agreed. It would be my final sacrifice. Then—quite firmly—I would quit. Hand in my resignation. I'd be outta there.

On Saturday morning, mothers deposited angels, wise men, shepherds and donkeys. The dress rehearsal went poorly. The donkey girl got a sliver in her knee, an angel wept over a broken halo, and the shepherds engaged in an unholy brawl. I popped two more aspirin and shouted directions across the noisy room.

That night, my stomach churned. From backstage I spotted . . . *him* . . . the cute guy, in the front row. And

I . . . very deliberately . . . stuck out my tongue. He didn't see me—but the minister did.

The minute the curtain opened, my seven-year-olds were magically transformed. Shepherds, heads swathed in terry towels, stood ramrod straight. Mary and Joseph knelt; angels heralded; wise men worshipped; donkeys . . . well, *everything* couldn't be perfect.

Except, maybe their voices.

"Si-i-lent night," the little ones serenaded.

"Ho-o-ly night," their sweet voices floated and filled the room.

"All is calm . . ." Sweeping the stage with a glance, I nodded in agreement. All *was* calm. And perfect.

Just like them.

By the end of the performance, I figured the gigantic lump in my throat might disfigure me for life. But, hey, I would learn to deal with it.

"Miss Whitley! Miss Whitley!" Matthew held onto his lopsided crown with one hand and a shoebox with the other. "My mom and dad came to see me! *Both* of them!"

"Both of them?" I marveled. I knew a neighbor brought lonely little Matthew to Sunday school each week. His divorced parents didn't have time.

"Miss Whitley," he tugged my arm for attention, "can I be in your class again next year?"

Ahhh, what a cute little fella.

And I agreed. On the spot.

"And, uh . . . Miss Whitley . . . thanks." He shoved the shoebox toward me. "For you." He ran to join his parents while I lifted the lid.

Oops.

But even as I stared at the ugly gift inside—aren't all grasshoppers ugly?—I recognized the love in a little boy's gratitude.

Someone walked near me and whispered, "God bless you, Miss Whitley, and thank you."

I glanced up at Mr. Cute and shot him a foolish smile.

"Thank *you*," I said. And meant it.

Sharon Whitley Larsen

READER/CUSTOMER CARE SURVEY

We care about your opinions! Please take a moment to fill out our online Reader Survey at **http://survey.hcibooks.com.**
As a **"THANK YOU"** you will receive a **VALUABLE INSTANT COUPON** towards future book purchases as well as a **SPECIAL GIFT** available only online! Or, you may mail this card back to us and we will send you a copy of our exciting catalog with your valuable coupon inside.
(PLEASE PRINT IN ALL CAPS)

First Name	M.I.	Last Name

Address		City

State	Zip	Email

1. Gender
❏ Female ❏ Male

2. Age
❏ 8 or younger
❏ 9-12 ❏ 13-16
❏ 17-20 ❏ 21-30
❏ 31+

3. Did you receive this book as a gift?
❏ Yes ❏ No

4. Annual Household Income
❏ under $25,000
❏ $25,000 - $34,999
❏ $35,000 - $49,999
❏ $50,000 - $74,999
❏ over $75,000

5. What are the ages of the children living in your house?
❏ 0 - 14 ❏ 15+

6. Marital Status
❏ Single
❏ Married
❏ Divorced
❏ Widowed

7. How did you find out about the book?
(please choose one)
❏ Recommendation
❏ Store Display
❏ Online
❏ Catalog/Mailing
❏ Interview/Review

8. Where do you usually buy books?
(please choose one)
❏ Bookstore
❏ Online
❏ Book Club/Mail Order
❏ Price Club (Sam's Club, Costco's, etc.)
❏ Retail Store (Target, Wal-Mart, etc.)

9. What subject do you enjoy reading about the most?
(please choose one)
❏ Parenting/Family
❏ Relationships
❏ Recovery/Addictions
❏ Health/Nutrition

❏ Christianity
❏ Spirituality/Inspiration
❏ Business Self-help
❏ Women's Issues
❏ Sports

10. What attracts you most to a book?
(please choose one)
❏ Title
❏ Cover Design
❏ Author
❏ Content

Chicken Soup for the Soul®
3201 SW 15th Street
Deerfield Beach FL 33442-9875

FOLD HERE

Do you have your own Chicken Soup story
that you would like to send us?
Please submit at: **www.chickensoup.com**

Comments

It's in the Mail

Spend some quiet time recalling the people who have impacted your life. Consider your first boss, your last roommate, Little League coaches and the high school janitor. Give some thought to religious leaders, best friends, over-the-fence neighbors, reliable garbage collectors, elderly aunts, music instructors, college professors and old classmates. Think outside the holiday box!

Next, choose four—one person per week—to acknowledge during December.

Under each of their names, list how they affected your life. Did she alter your course? Did he set a fine example? Did they help you through a crisis?

Now, send handwritten notes of appreciation—long ones. Be specific. Tell them why they matter and, above all, remember to say, "Thank you."

Faith

By Leaps and Mounds

You've heard it said; we all have. The odds are good that you've even said it yourself at one time or another: "Seeing is believing."

In the movie, *The Santa Clause*, Elf Judy put it another way: "Seeing isn't believing; believing is seeing."

And, of course, the Bible repeats the theme in renowned poetic perfection: "Faith is the substance of things hoped for, the evidence of things not seen" (Hebrews 11:1).

The world runs on faith. Wispy, yet tenacious. Universal, but personal. Effortless and, sometimes, arduous. Incorporating this virtue into our lives draws us into a larger, divine order.

Defined as "believing" and "trusting," faith is—above all else—an action, one we practice nearly every moment of our lives. Our belief or trust is automatic on the most basic human level. In a secular sense, we live by faith every day—from the magnificent to the mundane—by relying on the goodness of mankind, the principle of gravity, the diagnoses of physicians, even the descriptions in an encyclopedia.

On a more spiritual level, faith means taking chances. And nowhere is that more obvious than watching a child. Any child. Because that's where faith shines brightest—in a childlike heart.

Like Diane's.

After bouts of friendly water warfare, showing off their underwater handstands and playing shark, the kids were excited that their dad offered to take them to the other end of the swimming pool. The water there was so deep even Daddy couldn't touch the bottom.

"Let's try out the diving board," he urged.

Eight-year-old Kent scooted up the ladder, raced the length of the board and belly flopped into a splash that surprised even Daddy. Diane held back while her younger sister climbed the ladder and, with only a bit of coaxing, took hesitant steps to the edge. Wanda gave one half-hearted bounce, flung her arms upward in complete abandon and practically threw herself into Daddy's open arms.

"Your turn, punkin'."

Diane counted the five steps on the ladder. Twice. Once going up—and again scurrying down.

"Don't be afraid," Daddy called.

Even though her knees buckled, Diane made it up the ladder at last. She sidled the length of the diving board and curled her toes in a death grip over the edge. Wet and shivering, lips quivering, teeth chattering, she looked down, down . . . down to where Daddy treaded.

"I'll catch you," Daddy reassured her.

And Diane trusted. She leapt. Right into his arms.

Sometimes we must dare our souls to go further than is comfortable, further—at times—than we can see. That's how we practice faith; we actually create more faith—stronger faith—by trusting. In Daddy. In ourselves. In God. And to trust is, of course, to triumph.

And so it is that catchphrases abound, reminding us to build our faith:

Keep the faith.
Feed your faith.
Have faith.
Faith moves mountains.

As we exercise our faith, our lives grow stronger. We build our faith into muscle. And it becomes progressively easier to exercise trust and to believe. To realize dreams, achieve goals and fulfill ambitions.

Until, somewhere along the journey, we learn that an all-encompassing faith is our passport to joy.

Everybody Loves Santa

One Christmas season I helped Santa Claus by filling in for him at a small shopping mall. Instead of the usual assembly line of children, I enjoyed spontaneous visits with little tots bearing lists of toys, as well as the occasional surprise visits with teenagers and adults.

A bright, happy and chatty three-and-a-half-year-old sat on my lap, asking questions and answering mine. Finally, looking me in the eye, she said, "I thought you were fake. You're real!" Her doubts removed, I'm sure she had a magical Christmas.

A pair of fifteen-year-old boys ran up, hugged me lovingly and, grinning, asked, "Will you bring us each a motorcycle?" After a brief chat, they walked away chuckling.

A young father paid the elf photographer for a single picture. "I don't have custody of my children," he explained, "and I want to show them a picture of you and me shaking hands." He received the finished photo, mouthed "thank you" and left.

Three teenage girls skipped and twirled over. Giggling, one teased, "I want a sports car."

The second one topped her. "I want a mansion."

The last girl whispered in my ear, "I'd like a job for my dad."

As they walked away, her friends probed, "What did you ask for?"

"That's between me and Santa," she sighed.

Substitute Santa swallowed hard and wiped his eyes with his handkerchief. I truly believe the girl's father found a job becuse, you see, that night Santa prayed he would.

Robert H. Bickmeyer

Presence and Accounted For

Every gift had been wrapped, each recipe prepared, and all the ornaments hung. I had seen to every detail; I knew I hadn't overlooked a thing. And now, with my three anxious children tucked in bed at last, I leaned back in my favorite recliner—satisfied—to survey our perfect, shimmering tree.

I admired the gay packages arranged meticulously underneath. Thanks to my early planning and a little extra money this year, Christmas was going to be wonderful. I couldn't wait to see my children's faces when they tore into their presents the next morning, discovering all of the new clothes and great toys I had bought for them.

I began a mental accounting of the treasures tucked inside each package: the Dallas Cowboys jacket for Brandon, the Fisher Price castle for Jared, the Victorian dollhouse for Brittany . . .

Basking in the glow of twinkling lights and my own thoughts, I barely noticed Jared sneak into the room. My

normal reaction would be to jump up and rush him back to bed. Languidly curious this time, I chose to sit still and watch, hoping he wouldn't notice my presence.

I needn't have worried.

Jared was a five-year-old with a mission. The glimmering tree illuminated his small figure as he made his way straight to the nativity beneath it. Sinking to his knees, he held out a paper and whispered, "See, Jesus, I drew this picture for you."

Not wanting to miss a word, I held my breath and leaned forward.

"On the left side, that's me." Jared's finger traced a path across the page. "On the right side, that's you." He pointed. "In the middle is my heart." He smiled sweetly. "I'm giving it to you."

With tenderness, Jared placed the picture beneath the tree.

"Merry Christmas, Jesus," he said and scurried back to bed.

My throat tightened, and my eyes filled. All the sparkling decorations and all the shiny wrappings in the room suddenly dulled in comparison to Jared's innocent crayon drawing. It took my small child's gift of love to remind me that only Jesus can make Christmas wonderful this year. And he always does.

Vickie Ryan Koehler

Let's Get Real

For years and years, our family celebrated Christmas with an artificial tree. The tradition caught on during the seventies when we were living in Australia and it was *hotter'n all get-out* during the month of December. While the Aussies smothered themselves with zinc cream as they sunbaked on the beach, our family held tenaciously to its American customs, insisting on a traditional sit-down Christmas dinner and, of course, a real-looking tree.

Unfortunately, the heat was too extreme to trust an evergreen, and those who did were soon sorry. Fearing a not-so-festive display of bare branches or, worse yet, a house fire, we opted for the artificial. White plastic, to be exact.

"It looks gross," my kids whined.

And try as we might to cover it with handmade or imported ornaments, it somehow never made the grade. Meanwhile, year after year, we piled our gifts underneath the fake tree—never even noticing that, with age, it had slowly turned yellow.

Our first yuletide back in America was electric. Dallas, Texas, was never billed as Christmas-in-Vermont, but the possibilities were everywhere. Nurseries from Plano to Waco showcased a winter wonderland of snow-flocked, bushy Scotch pines. Roadside stands, advertised solely by a single strand of swinging lightbulbs, beckoned at dusk for highway travelers to stop and shop in a forest of firs. And supermarkets all around the city did their bit by offering a variety of spruce and cedars to their customers.

Once again, we considered the possibility of buying a *real* tree. Having discarded our white plastic tradition on a friend's doorstep when we left Australia, our kids had high hopes that America could make all their dreams come true. But eventually, dreams gave way to budget, and we hauled home yet another inexpensive imitation.

"At least this one is green," I told them, "and besides, we won't have the repeated cost of buying a freshly cut tree every Christmas."

So, for the next fifteen years, we piled our gifts beneath the branches of a manufactured pine—never even noticing that, with age, it had slowly lost its beauty.

This year, however, something magical took place. It happened one night as I approached the electronic doors of our neighborhood grocery store. Out of the corner of my eye, I spied a breathtakingly beautiful, real-live Christmas tree, leaning near the entrance. It was there with all the others, yet standing apart. I made a detour to take a second look.

The grand fir that caught my attention stood ten feet high. It was indeed a lofty tree, and I ran my fingers over the needles, surprised by their softness.

Hmmm, maybe this is why children love real trees at Christmas,
I thought, smelling the woodsy fragrance in the air.

A store clerk was working at the far end, slowly watering
the trees and making his way in my direction. But I was in
no hurry, so I waited. When he saw me admiring the fir, he
called out, "Hey, great tree for hanging ornaments!"

I acknowledged him by waving and stepping back to
make my final decision. At that very moment, a pre-
recorded Christmas carol cascaded through the sound
system, out into the night. Customers rushed past—some
going in, some going out—more or less oblivious to the
majestic music filling the air. And the words spilled across
the busy parking lot, "No-el, No-el, No-el, No-el. Born is
the king of Is-rael," to the accompaniment of a Salvation
Army bell ringer just outside the door.

As I stood in the shadow of that noble fir, I knew this
was the year I needed to buy a *real* tree. For no other reason than this is a *real* story being told, a *real* message being
sung, and a *real* occasion to celebrate.

So this year, for the very first time ever, our family will
pile all our Christmas gifts underneath a towering noble
fir—never even noticing that, with age, we're slowly
becoming believers all over again.

Charlotte A. Lanham

Ho, Ho, Hope

My decision in the 1960s to run away from a newly divorced life in California and move to the safety of Canada was a big one—one I had to think over for nearly five minutes.

Hooking a battered trailer to my ancient Chevy, I gathered my five young children and headed for parts unknown. Along with my little brood, I took a month's worth of rent money, a pocketful of dreams, some hope for our future and a heart filled with faith.

Vulnerable and haggard after the long drive, I slowed my rickety rig when I saw the sign ahead. With five tousled heads bobbing in the windows, the startled border guard's mouth flew open.

My seven-year-old tossed him her cheekiest smile. One six-year-old twin looked tremulous and wide-eyed at the large man brandishing a gun on his hip; the other glared in defiance. My two- and three-year-old toddlers babbled to capture his attention and interest him in their toy cars and stuffed animals.

Obviously, we'd caught the bewildered guard . . . *off guard.*

Warning that I'd better have a job (I did) and threatening immediate deportation if I attempted to go on welfare, he waved us through.

Shortly after we settled in a small apartment, my old car sputtered to a quick death. I found a sitter for the children and began hitchhiking to work, but because I was sometimes late, I lost the job. My last check went for another month's rent, and there was nothing left for food. As Christmas approached, desperation dogged every waking minute and even disturbed my sleep.

So did the kids' concerns.

"Is Santa *real*, Momma?"

"Will he find us, Momma?"

"Do you believe in him, Momma?"

With painstaking care, I explained that Santa didn't know where we'd moved and would miss us this year, but we had each other, and we would make do and . . . sing Christmas songs and . . . try making gifts and . . . and . . . well, everything would work out.

So, even without a tree, we glued colored paper garlands and strung popcorn to make the apartment festive and ourselves cheerful.

But the day before Christmas, my desperation reached a new low: We had nothing in the cupboard for supper. Reluctantly, I approached our neighbor and asked to borrow a can or two of soup to feed my children. After a curt "No," the door slammed in my face.

Humiliation and shame were my new companions.

And, for the first time in my life, I felt utter fear, despair and hopelessness.

Christmas Eve, I drew my little ones near—the boys on my lap, the girls nestled at my sides. In our meagerly decorated room, we told stories, played games and sang seasonal songs. I smiled at my wee darlings, but inside I was crying. And praying, again and again.

Please, God, oh please, God, send us help.

A sudden, loud *THUMP* at the door startled us all.

"Ho, ho, ho!" A hearty voice accompanied a loud knock.

And there in our doorway stood the jolly old man himself!

With a full sack slung over his back and three merry elves crowding his sides, Santa Claus brought the excitement of Christmas into our small home. He came bearing all kinds of wonderful gifts, something special for each child. Plus, an assortment of toys, games and books—even a gift for me—appeared from the depths of his deep pack! Christmas dinner (courtesy of the Vancouver Fire Department) was included, as well: turkey and the trimmings, enough to last several days.

Laughing and crying, I gazed around the joy-filled room at the satisfied faces of Santa and his helpers and the gleeful abandonment of my little family.

"Momma, Momma, he's real!" they chorused. "Santa found us!"

Yes, indeed he found us . . . in answer to my prayer. And that made a believer out of me.

Angela Hall

Away from the Manger

"Okay, that's the last of it." Michael stacked the final box in my entry hall.

I surveyed the tattered, dusty containers with anticipation. To me, these Christmas decorations from Michael's childhood, in storage since his mother's death, signified our future together as a couple. We were sharing all sorts of holiday activities—parties, shopping and, now, decorating. In a few months we'd be married, and I was eager to create some traditions of our own. I yearned for meaningful practices, significant and unique to the two of us.

Opening the crates was a start.

"Hey, here's our old nativity set." Michael pulled out a well-packed box. "Mom always put it under the Christmas tree."

I carefully unwrapped Mary and Joseph and the manger. Stuffed deep in the newspapers was a stable. I placed it on the floor beneath the tree and arranged three wise men, a shepherd boy, a lamb and a cow. All accounted for, except . . .

I double-checked the loose packing and looked under the wadded newspapers, hoping to find the missing figure. Nothing.

"Honey," I called to Michael, who was busily arranging Santa's toyshop in the dining room. "I can't find Jesus."

Walking to my side, he playfully squeezed my shoulder. "Excuse me?"

"The baby Jesus for the nativity. He's not here!" I rummaged through more wrappings.

Michael's expression tensed. "He's here. He has to be. He was here the last Christmas Mom was alive."

Hours later, all the boxes were unpacked, but Jesus never appeared. Michael regretfully suggested we pack the nativity scene back in the crate.

"No," I said. "I'll find a baby that matches the set tomorrow."

We kissed good night, and Michael went home.

The next day, I stuffed the manger into my purse and headed to the hobby store during my lunch hour. No Jesus there. After work, I searched for him at several other stores only to discover that baby Jesus *wasn't sold separately*. I considered buying another nativity just to replace the Jesus in Michael's, but none of the infants fit the manger.

Michael arrived for dinner a few days later, and I broke the news to him. After we ate, I began to repack the figurines in their box. Michael stilled my hands with his.

"I think we should leave it up."

"Honey, we can't. There's no baby," I replied. "We can't have a nativity without Jesus."

"Wait a minute." Michael pulled me away from the tree. "Now look from back here."

He pointed. "At first glance, you don't notice anything missing. It's not until you look closely that you see the Christ Child is gone."

I cocked my head and looked at the scene. He was right. "But I don't get your point."

"Amid the decorations, shopping lists and parties, sometimes we lose sight of Jesus," he explained. "Somehow, he gets lost in the midst of Christmas."

And then I understood.

So began our first Christmas tradition—significant and unique to our family. Each year, we position the treasured figures in their customary places. The manger remains empty. It's our gentle reminder to look for Christ at Christmas.

Stephanie Welcher Thompson

The Family Tree

"Mr. Zimmerman's sons are returning home to take over the farm."

The adult conversation around the kitchen table worried me. At seven years old, I was big enough to understand what that meant: My father and brother would no longer be working for the German farmer, and that spelled disaster.

The Great Depression had hit our rural Idaho community, and money was scarce that Christmas. Most of Father's income from Mr. Zimmerman was in trade for food and a place to live. This place. The only home I'd ever known. The home I loved.

The two-story farmhouse had one large sleeping room upstairs. It opened to a balcony overlooking the backyard and my favorite oak tree. During the spring and summer, soft, warm breezes blew through the room, and Jimmy, Eddie, Iris and I played for hours on end.

Now it was too cold. We had closed off the upstairs for everything but sleeping. Most of our winter living was done downstairs next to the warm fireplace, or in the kitchen where Mother was always baking yeasty breads and fragrant pies.

I was sitting on the floor playing with Harley, who was learning to crawl, when mother came in from the pump and set the bucket on the large woodstove. Water sloshed onto the hot stovetop, sizzling and filling the air with steam.

"Mother, will we really have to leave here?" My question was blunt. It was the worry foremost in my mind.

She looked down at me, sympathy and understanding etching her kind face. "Yes, Carol, we will."

I frowned. "But what about Christmas?"

"It will be the last holiday we'll celebrate in this house." Mother verbalized my darkest fear.

"And a tree? Will we have a tree?"

"Child, we have no means to get a tree this year."

But I couldn't—I wouldn't—accept her calm answer. Somehow we *must* have a tree for our last family Christmas in this wonderful old farmhouse.

That night I prayed for a very, very long time.

The next morning I hurried downstairs fully expecting to see the answer to my prayers, but there was no tree. I put on my warm sweater and mittens and headed to the outhouse. As the cold air hit my face, I became even more determined.

When Father left to walk the four miles into town, I decided to wait outside until he returned—even if it took all day. I settled beneath my favorite oak on the cold, hard ground, certain he'd bring home a tree.

It seemed like I'd been sitting for hours when I felt the

ground start to rumble and heard a dull, distant roar that grew louder and louder. I jumped to my feet and ran to the fence. A large truck—full of Christmas trees—was headed for delivery in the city. My heart pounded as it drew up beside our house.

And then, like a hand tossing them from heaven, two large branches flew right off the truck and bounced into our front yard. My prayers had been answered. My tree had arrived!

I raced inside and, my words tripping over each other, babbled to Mother about how badly I wanted a tree for our last Christmas here and how hard I had prayed for it and how I was hoping Father would bring one home and how I just *knew* we'd get one in time for Christmas and now . . . and *now!*

Mother took my hand and walked me outside where Iris, Jimmy and Eddie stood gawking at the miracle in our yard. She smiled and pulled us together in a hug. "And to think, children, it was Carol's faith that brought us our tree."

We tied the bushy limbs together, then decorated them with wallpaper scraps and garlands of popcorn. I admired the tree as it stood in our big farmhouse home and knew it was the most beautiful tree I'd ever seen.

That year I also received the only doll I would ever have as a child. But my greatest gift was the discovery that—with faith—miracles happen.

Carol Keim
As told to (daughter) Tamara Chilla
Submitted by (niece) Laura Linares

Going Global

Hoping for a white Christmas? Why not create a wintry scene straight from your own imagination by designing a holiday snow globe?

Supplies you'll need:

- any small, clean jar (jelly, pimento, olive, baby food, etc.)
- miniature figurines (synthetic, plastic or ceramic) from hobby stores, cake-supply centers or model-railroad shops
- clear-drying epoxy
- distilled water
- glycerin (purchase at any pharmacy)
- glitter

How to:

- Roughen the inside of the jar lid with an emery board or sand paper.
- Adhere the figurines to the inside of the lid with epoxy and let it dry.
- Fill the jar almost full with distilled water.
- Add a pinch or two of glitter for "snow."
- Pour in a dash of glycerin (to slow the glitter).
- Screw the lid on tightly, and seal it with epoxy.

Now, turn the jar upside down, and—let it snow!

Wonder

Wonder Full

The true path to Christmas, it is said, lies through an ancient gate.

And, according to the sages, the gate is child-wide and child-high, and the secret password is a childlike sigh. A sigh of wonder.

Come, take my hand. Bend low and slip through the arbor for a glimpse of Mother Nature at her most generous: into the lush hush of Christmas in the Rockies . . . where pinions sprawl, ponderosas slumber and bristlecones snuggle in quiet companionship. Where spruce trees—too green to be black, yet too black to be green—pace the perimeters of the forest glade like expectant fathers. Where cobalt shadows float, mysterious and beckoning, beneath supple pines while winter's wind breathes hints of miracles to come.

Billowing whiteness greets us and glistens under wide winter heavens, star-studded with promise to chase away the dark. Each intricately petaled snowflake is food for rambling thought and fancy; pieced together, they make a downy coverlet that wraps us with anticipation.

Above this scene, a sliver of divinity crowns the night sky, spikes mounds of snow with intoxicating moonshine and then, satisfied, preens itself in the mirrored skin of a crystal mountain lake. And, all the while, stellar luminaries capture this pristine image in a series of freeze-framed moments—an album of memories to treasure.

Even as it scours the warmth from our days, winter plies us with tender gestures—if we seek them. As Henry David Thoreau once said, "The question is not what you look at, but what you see."

What do we choose to see in winter? Icy porches, slushy sidewalks, a drive to shovel? Or is our vision filled with eye-catching "still lifes" and Currier-and-Ives vistas?

How do we let wonder weave its way into our thoughts? How do we convince it to replace indifference, detachment and apathy?

It's simple. Watch a small child. Spend time with a child. Take a child's hand in yours, walk through the fabled gate... and witness the miracle of discovery and endless possibilities.

A child sees a skating rink on every icy porch.

A child sees puddle possibilities in every slushy sidewalk.

A child sees snow angels to create, snow forts to construct, snowballs to roll and snowmen to build in every uncleared driveway.

Children are excitement seekers. They gravitate toward surprise, amazement, awe and astonishment. An air of expectancy swirls around them like hot chocolate. They hope. They marvel. They share a powerful belief that miracles happen. They live with a broader sense of wonder. They point out the beauty, the opportunities and the experiences we might otherwise miss.

At this yuletide season, perhaps more than any other, we can inhale the innocence of youth. We can see Christmas—and the world—through different eyes. We can seek out this treasure worth preserving. We can learn the virtue of wonder and rehearse it until it sings through our veins.

And we can do it by becoming more childlike. Recall the old poem, "Backward, turn backward, O Time, in your flight; make me a child again just for tonight" (Elizabeth Akers Allen). Take it to heart.

Let yourself be surprised. Don't be reluctant to express admiration or to exclaim in delight. Show enthusiasm. Practice joy. Spread ardor. Above all, look for magic and hope for miracles this Christmas. You'll find them on the wispy wings of wonder . . . just beyond the garden gate.

A Place of Honor

"Package for you, ma'am."

The postman left a plain box. It bore no printing, no hint as to the contents. Our overwhelming urge to shake the box produced only a slight shift in the load. Carefully cutting around the top, we removed the lid and peered inside.

With a questioning look on his face, my husband slowly unpacked six chubby figures and stood them on the table. When he placed a small, triangular bundle at their feet, I couldn't suppress a broad grin. Black, beady eyes, looking slightly myopic and a bit crossed, stared at us from under snatches of acrylic hair. With no noticeable change in their expressions, they stood quietly awaiting our inspection and approval.

Some months earlier I had mentioned to our daughter Kaye Lynn my desire to have a set of heavy-duty, child-proof nativity dolls for our grandchildren to enjoy. I wanted peace of mind when inquisitive little fingers felt a need to hold or examine one.

I also thought their own private collection would distract them from the stunning crèche ensemble I hoped to acquire. I dreamed of a lavish array of ceramic or porcelain, perhaps even crystal, to occupy a place of honor in our home—a spot where Mary and Joseph could display their precious babe undisturbed. Each piece would stand amid ripples of gold lamé fabric, the bright glow of carefully directed lights reflecting off polished surfaces.

My husband and I giggled as we examined each little guest. A more comical group of adoring subjects I had never imagined! They had been crafted with a wild sense of humor and a practical streak as well. For instance, contrary to popular belief, a blonde Mary wore crisp, pink-and-white gingham—easy to launder, cool in a desert climate and ultrafeminine. Joseph, on the other hand, appeared dapper in his brown plaid—ideal for traveling the dusty roads of Judea. His flowing auburn hair and full beard lent an air of sophistication.

I imagined an audible sigh of relief as we unfurled the angel's white felt wings that had been tucked tightly around her body. Her embroidered eyes were stitched closed, either in reverence or perhaps fatigue after her busy night proclaiming the wondrous news. And baby Jesus slept through it all, an odd little three-inch package swaddled in blue felt, glued atop a pile of old-fashioned excelsior packing.

There were no shepherds. No doubt they left early, anxious to spread the joyous word; besides, they had sheep to tend. Robed in plush fabric, three wise men wore identical silver hats. No knees bent in adoration; their fat little bodies were not designed for that.

The unexpected gift became a cherished possession.

Our grandchildren love those little people. Each doll has been hugged and kissed and taken on walking tours throughout the house. Secrets have been whispered and bruised feelings healed as they rocked together.

Baby Jesus has enjoyed many a quiet nap under the sofa, in a drawer or on someone's bed. Joseph never complains when his long hair is brushed and braided, parted and ponytailed as little girls practice their tonsorial skills. To our delight, one of the grandchildren recently dubbed the wise men "those three old guys in the shower caps."

The dolls survive all this affection remarkably well. Their wire arms assume astonishing positions, but they're still flexible. The excelsior hay dried and broke off, but a handful of pale yarn works just fine—and baby Jesus slept right through the regluing. The angel's droopy wings need to be replaced with new white felt. At this rate, the set will be in fine shape for our great-grandchildren.

And my burning desire for an impressive crèche subsided. Our daughter Barbara displayed hers atop the piano while they lived with us—gold lamé, bright lights and all. When she moved, she not only took her porcelain figurines, but five grandchildren and the piano as well.

We were left with only our little stuffed dolls, and it was okay.

Recently, the delivery service left another brown cardboard box. It was huge and much too big to shake. How exciting to remove packing by the yard, boxes inside boxes, with Bubble-Pak® and cotton batting stuffed everywhere.

This time we unwrapped ceramic sheep and shepherds,

cows and camels, donkeys and wise men (some of which *are* kneeling), and the holy family. Kaye Lynn had hand-painted them all, and they are beautiful.

Now, I must give some thought as to where I can best display the cast and characters of my new crèche. I want them to represent the peace of the season and the rich-ness of its message—but with a bit of flair. And I also want them to be safe from curious little fingers. Which location will I designate as the "place of honor"?

On second thought, maybe that spot has already been chosen.

Is there a lovelier place than in the chubby arms of a child? Can gold lamé shine as brightly as the eyes of a toddler as he sings to his "baby"—even if it is a wise man? Do spotlights and crystal compare to the light of Christmas shining in the face of innocence as a grand-daughter and Mary share a moment in deep discussion about parenting skills?

Those first fat, little dolls with their fake hair and poor eyesight have been in the place of honor all this time, and I never realized it.

Now if I can just remember to buy some new white felt!

Mary Kerr Danielson

The Lone Caroler

The mall's parking garage was so packed that we had to drive around and around, up and down several levels, before we found a space. Of course, I should have expected as much. After all, this was the week before Christmas at the busiest shopping mall in the county.

Jumping out of the car, I held tight to my purse in one hand and my shopping list in the other. Screeching brakes, tooting horns, shouting customers, banging trunk lids, gunning motors, blaring loudspeaker music—what clamor! I could hardly think. And I certainly needed to think straight to plan my mad dashes from store to store. So much to do and so little time in which to do it.

As I rushed to the garage elevator, somehow through all that noise I heard a strange *chrrr, chrrr*. It almost had a rhythm to it. But where was the sound coming from?

Looking up, I saw a hole in the garage wall. Nestled inside was a small brown bird, shaped like a chickadee, but more sparrowlike in color. In fact, contrasted against all the red and green and gold of the season, the bird was absolutely dull and ordinary. To look at, that is, but not to listen to. The tiny creature was singing its heart out.

Chrrr, chrrr . . .

There, among the jarring sounds of racing cars and people, I realized it was responding to music on the loudspeaker. A Christmas carol? Why, yes—"Silent Night."

Though I was very close to him now, he didn't try to fly, but kept pouring out his heart with complete abandon. Perfect in rhythm and pitch, he syncopated each measure of the three-quarter-time melody, coming in only on the last two beats. As in, "Si- *(chrrr, chrrr)*, night *(chrrr, chrrr)*, ho- *(chrrr, chrrr)*, night *(chrrr, chrrr)*." Almost calypso style.

I didn't recognize his species. Many kinds of birds winter here in Southern California, and I'm not a "birder." But in the crowded parking garage that day, he alone took time to rejoice in and praise the reason for the season.

So I stopped and joined him.

He didn't seem to mind the cars whizzing by us or that my voice was cracked and weak and off-key. Never had "sleep in heavenly peace" seemed so out of place; it was neither night nor silent.

Only when the carol ended did we both hurry off to our respective duties. But as I headed into the jam-packed mall, I, too, had wings. And a glowing smile. "Christ our savior is born." Hallelujah!

Bonnie Compton Hanson

The Right Touch

It was four days before Christmas and the town sat still, as if Old Man Winter had forgotten the snow everyone was wishing for.

Grandpa and I worked at the department store where he asked kids what they wanted for Christmas while I distributed candy canes and small presents. Grandpa's beard was real, bushy and full. Some of the kids who tugged it were quite surprised. And when he ho ho–ed, his stomach shook. Grandpa *was* Santa Claus, no question.

Most of the lap-sitters were under ten. They were pretty much alike, asking for bikes, dolls, radios and games. But one little girl was different. Her mother led her up, and Grandpa hoisted her onto his lap. Her name was Tina. She was blind.

"What do you want for Christmas, Tina?" Grandpa asked.

"Snow," she answered shyly.

Grandpa smiled. His eyes twinkled. "Well, I'll see what I can do about that. But how about something just for you? Something special?"

Tina hesitated and whispered in Grandpa's ear. I saw a smile creep over his face.

"Sure, Tina," was all he said.

He took her hands in his and placed them on his cheeks. His eyes drifted shut, and he sat there smiling as the girl began to sculpt his face with her fingers. She paused here and there to linger, paying close attention to every wrinkle and whisker. Her fingers seemed to be memorizing the laugh lines under Grandpa's eyes and at the corners of his mouth. She stroked his beard and rolled its wiry ringlets between her thumbs and forefingers. When she finished, she paused to rest her palms on Grandpa's shoulders.

He opened his eyes. They were twinkling.

Suddenly her arms flew out, encircling Grandpa's neck in a crushing hug. "Oh, Santa," she cried. "You look just like I knew you did. You're perfect, just perfect."

As Tina's mother lifted her down from his lap, Grandpa smiled, then blinked, and a tear rolled down his cheek.

That night when my grandmother came to pick us up, I watched her help Grandpa transfer into his wheelchair and position his limp legs on the footrests. "So, Santa," she winked, "how was your day?"

He looked up at me and pressed his lips together. Then he looked at Grandma, cleared his throat, and said with a tiny smile, "Sweetheart, it was perfect, just perfect."

Outside it began to snow.

Steve Burt

Christmas Derailed

Boxes, ribbons and wrappings cluttered the entire room, evidence of a rowdy but generous Christmas morning for five-year-old Christopher and his three-year-old brother, David. But Christopher was far too withdrawn and quiet for a little boy who had just received his first electric train set. A bit concerned, I kept watch from the corner of my maternal eye while I scrambled eggs, maintained a running conversation with Grandma and periodically hauled Blossom, our bumbling sheepdog, away from the now listing tree.

What could be wrong? I wondered. Tummy ache? Christopher wasn't complaining. Disappointment? Not likely, considering his ecstatic response when he saw the train set. Annoyed by the toddling interference of his little brother? No, David played across the room, chattering incessantly to his grandpa and daddy.

Yet I knew a mysterious, dark cloud hung over Christopher's mood this Christmas morning and carved a furrow of deep thought across his forehead. What in the

world was making him so sad and dejected? Unable to find a moment alone with him in all the holiday chaos, I worried as he periodically retreated to his room, only to reappear with the same gloomy look.

When the breakfast dishes were finally put away, and the rest of the family had settled into the quiet hum of conversation and coffee, I took my cup of tea and slid to the floor next to Christopher, where he distractedly spun a wheel on one of his new trucks.

"Hey, honey," I whispered quietly in his ear, "I noticed that you seem a little sad this morning. What's wrong?"

"Well, Mommy," he said in a melancholy little voice, "remember that ring I got in the gumball machine? I gave it to the Tooth Fairy for Christmas."

Oh no, I groaned inwardly.

"How did you do that?" I asked, with a foreboding sense of what I was about to hear.

"Oh, I put it under my pillow where she always looks. But she didn't take it. I been checking all morning, and it's still there. And I really wanted to give her a present. How come she didn't want it?" he asked plaintively, looking up at me for an answer.

Rejected by the Tooth Fairy! How could she have been so thoughtless? And how could I explain without completely deflating the faith and kind heart of this little boy?

"Hmmm," I stalled. "Do you think she's busy collecting teeth this morning? Maybe she'll come later."

He considered the possibility thoughtfully, but shook his head. "No, I don't think so. She comes at night when kids are asleep."

I had to make this right. But how? Moments passed

while I groped for another idea—any idea. Then, quite unexpectedly, Christopher's entire being erupted with eureka joy.

"Mommy, I bet I know why she didn't take it!" he blurted. "I bet she's Jewish!" And with that resolved, off he ran, smiling broadly, to engineer his new electric train.

Armené Humber

Troubled

A song sung by Faith Hill in the blockbuster movie *The Grinch* asks: "Where are you, Christmas? Why can't I find you?" Well, sometimes the Christmas spirit is like a misplaced sock—you find it when you aren't looking and where you'd least expect it to show up.

I found it at a quarter past one in the morning.

On my way home from work, I stopped at the neighborhood doughnut shop. After parking in its ghost town of a parking lot, I was headed toward the door when I spotted trouble.

What lit a warning light on my intuition radar was a group of teenagers—three boys and a girl. Understand, I wasn't alarmed by their tattoos (the girl included) or their earrings (boys included—eyebrows as well as each of their ears). Rather, it was the extremely late hour and the fact they loitered on the sidewalk in a semicircle around an elderly man sitting in a chair. Wearing a tattered flannel shirt and barefoot, the man looked positively cold and probably homeless.

And in trouble with a capital T.

Against my better judgment, I went inside the store and ordered three doughnuts—while keeping a worried eye on the group outside. Nothing seemed to be happening.

Until I headed toward my car.

Something was indeed "going down." As ominously as a pirate ordering a prisoner to the plank, the teens told the old man to stand up and walk.

Oh, no, I thought. *Capital tee-are-oh-you-bee-el-ee.*

But wait. I had misjudged the situation. And I had misjudged the teens.

"How do those feel?" one of the boys asked. "Do they fit?"

The cold man took a few steps—maybe a dozen. He stopped, looked at his feet, turned around and walked back. "Yeah, they'z about my size," he answered, flashing a smile that, despite needing a dentist's attention, was friendly and warm on this cold night.

The teens, all four, grinned back.

"Keep them. They're yours," one of the boys replied. "I want you to have them."

I looked down. The teen was barefoot. The kid had just given the cold-and-probably-homeless man his expensive skateboarding sneakers—and, apparently his socks, as well.

The other two boys sat on their skateboards by the curb, retying their shoelaces. Apparently, they, too, had let the man try on their sneakers to find which pair fit the best. The girl, meanwhile, gave the cold man her oversized sweatshirt.

With my heart warmed by the unfolding drama, I went back into the shop.

"Could I trouble you for another dozen doughnuts?" I asked, then told the clerk what I had witnessed.

Christmas spirit, it seemed, was more contagious than flu or chicken pox. Indeed, the cold night got even warmer when the woman not only wouldn't let me pay for the doughnuts, but added a large coffee, too.

"These are from the lady inside. Have a nice night," I said as I delivered the warm doughnuts and piping-hot cup. The old man smiled appreciatively.

"You have a nice night, too," the teens said.

I already had.

Woody Woodburn

'Twas the Night

When I was a child, our family traditionally caroled on Christmas Eve. It was a joint venture, with the neighborhood churches all participating. Not only did we brave the cold winds to sing door-to-door, but our caroling benefited the Fannie Battle Day Home, a local organization for unwed mothers.

The procedure was routine. We met at the local Methodist church, divided into teams and conducted a quick rehearsal. A child was commissioned as spokesperson for the evening and given a modest, wooden box with a slit in the top to collect donations.

Assuming a seven-year-old could easily pull the heartstrings of any Scrooge that lived in the district, someone handed *me* the collection box that year. My assignment was elementary: Wait patiently until someone opened the door, and then cheerfully announce, "Merry Christmas! We're collecting money for the Fannie Battle Day Home. Would you like to make a donation?"

I memorized my lines before leaving the church and

walked proudly ahead of the others, protecting the box with my tiny, gloved hands.

A dusty snow fell around us, and halos around the streetlamps provided our only light—except for the flashlights used to read music. Some houses felt inviting, others intimidating, but—sensing the choir was never far behind—I boldly approached each home and knocked loudly.

A towering old man, dressed in his pajamas, came to a window and peered through the curtains before opening his door. My knees trembled, but I waited until he acknowledged me and courageously blurted out my rehearsed appeal.

"Merry Christmas! We're from the Dannie Hattle Fay Bome. Would you like to make a monation?"

The man chuckled and motioned his wife to bring his wallet. Together they dropped in a few dollars. Ah, success! On to the next house.

"Merry Christmas! We're from the Hannie Dattle Bay Fome. Would you care to make a dolation?"

And at another door, "Merry Christmas! We're from the Bannie Fattle Hay Dome. Would you need to make some domations?"

No doubt about it, I was *cute*. And in spite of the fact that I couldn't get the words right, people were generous and good-hearted. But I was young and cold and growing weary.

Too tired to carry on, I surrendered my position at the front line of duty to a more experienced caroler. Huddling close to the others, I stomped my feet and blew my breath into my palms like I watched others do. It wasn't long before we arrived at the end of Cephas Avenue, completing the circle back to the Methodist Church.

Hot chocolate, doughnuts and my mother waited for us in the warm hall. Once my toes were thawed and my tummy full, Mama took me home and nestled me all snug in my wee little bed.

But there were no sugarplums dancing in my head that night. No visions of candy canes or lollipops. Instead, I fell asleep remembering the faces of those who gladly put money into my little wooden box . . . remembering the house where we sang around the bedside of a wrinkled, old lady in a hospital gown . . . remembering how she cried when we left . . . remembering the carolers softly singing "Away in a Manger" under a light snow.

The night's music and magic stayed with me. And I remember it still—each Christmas Eve—when I'm nestled all snug in my wee little bed.

Charlotte A. Lanham

Let It Snow!

"Wasn't tonight's church service wonderful, Beth?"

"Hmm? I'm sorry. What did you say, dear?"

Roe glanced at his wife. "I asked what you thought of the Christmas Eve program."

"Nice. It was . . . nice." Beth looked over her shoulder. All three kids slumped against each other in the backseat, sound asleep.

"But?"

Beth didn't answer. She turned to stare out the windshield. A steady stream of traffic slinked like a glowworm, inching its way along the interstate at the foothills of Colorado's Front Range.

"Beth? What's wrong?"

"Wrong? Oh, I'm not sure that anything in particular is wrong, but it's not exactly right, either." She sighed. "Or maybe it's just that everything is so . . . different."

"Well, this isn't Minnesota," Roe chuckled.

"No, it's not, and that's the problem. I guess I'm home-sick. Christmas in Minnesota was . . ." Beth's voice trailed off, and her mind followed.

Christmas—in Minnesota.

Where stars glittered over a frozen wonderland. How well she knew those winter scenes with steepled churches, fence posts, fields and barns. All covered with icy snow, wonderful for sledding and old-fashioned sleigh rides and building igloos and forts and massive snow sculptures and . . .

Christmas—at church.

Where friends whispered seasonal greetings. Where aunts, uncles and giggling young cousins crowded into pews. Where grandparents still sang the old carols in Norwegian.

Christmas—at home.

Where getting a tree meant a trip to the woods on the family farm and a lively debate over the merits of each person's chosen favorite. Where Grandpa's axe always made the first cut and the kids dragged the tree to the car by its trunk. Where sticky sap glued their mittens to the bark.

To her, Christmas was Minnesota. Her childhood was gift-wrapped in those warm memories of tradition, and she had planned on more of the same for her own kids. Until this move changed everything.

Instead, here they were, heading back to a new house in a new neighborhood after participating in a—different—Christmas Eve service with new people in a new church.

"I'm sorry, Roe. Tonight's program really went well. I

guess I just missed our traditional sing-a-long, bell choir and candlelight vespers."

"Different places do different things, Beth. You'll get used to it." Roe signaled to change lanes.

"I suppose."

"Truthfully, I think your homesickness is nothing that a good snowfall couldn't cure," Roe teased as he eased the car toward the exit ramp.

"Well, I must admit, when we moved here this autumn and I got my first glimpse of those towering Rocky Mountains, I just assumed snowy winters were a given." Beth looked at the dark peaks silhouetted against the clear night sky and shivered. "But all this cold weather and not a flake in sight!"

"Only in the upper elevations." Roe pointed to Long's Peak, favored hiking destination of the locals. "There's the nearest snow and plenty of it."

"A lot of good that does!"

"It's probably only a hour's drive to the trailhead. What do you say we head up there tomorrow with the kids and spend Christmas afternoon in the mountains?"

Beth grimaced. Spending part of Christmas Day driving to find snow didn't fit her mood, and it certainly didn't fill the mold of traditional holiday activities.

"It's not the same as shoveling sidewalks or building a snowman in the yard or making an arsenal." She paused. "Remember the snowball fights we used to have?"

Roe and Beth grinned at each other.

"Yeah," Roe said. "In fact, just today I was telling that nice Ben Johnston across the alley how much we'll miss the neighborhood snowball challenges we hosted in Minnesota each Christmas. He got a good chuckle when I told him it was kids against adults—and the adults usually lost."

"That's what I want for Christmas, Roe."

"What?"

"I want to look out the window Christmas morning and see something more than winter-brown grass. I want snow and an old-fashioned snowball fight with friends. Home *means* tradition. Is tradition too much to ask for?"

Slowing, Roe turned down Logan Drive.

"Oh, Beth, I'm sorry this move has been so rough on . . . Well, I'll be!" Roe braked in the middle of the street. "Look!"

Beth gasped. Their lawn—bare and brown only hours before—was covered with several inches of snow. The grass, the walks, the porch and the bushes all sparkled under the streetlight's glow.

"Snow, kids, snow! Wake up and look at our yard!"

Rubbing sleep from their eyes, all three kids tumbled from the car and raced to the glittery powder. Beth and Roe sat spellbound.

"I can't believe my eyes," said Beth. "Snow! SNOW! But . . . it's only in OUR yard. How? And . . . why?"

"Who knows, Hon? But you certainly got your Christmas wish, or part of it, anyway."

Roe pointed down the street. "Well, would you look at that!" Ben Johnston's muddied pickup—loaded with snowblowers and shovels, headlights dimmed—slipped around the corner, leaving a fine trail of white.

"And tomorrow you get the rest." He smiled at his wife. "What do you say we revive an old snowball tradition—with a brand-new neighborhood of friends!"

Carol McAdoo Rehme

Suitable for Flaming

The hearth is the natural gathering place for family celebrations, so why not implement the warm ritual of burning the Yule log? Don't have a fireplace? Don't let that keep you from participating. Select the method that works for your family.

Traditional:
Traipse to the woodpile and select the nicest log to burn this Christmas. Embellish it with sprigs of evergreen, holly leaves or mistletoe. Tie the bundle with a burnable holiday ribbon.

Alternative:
Drill a shallow hole in a short log and fill it with a scented candle. Decorate with seasonal ornaments, artificial snow or holiday ribbon.

Display your Yule log on the hearth, mantle or table until Christmas Eve. Then, with great ceremony, light or burn your log, sing "Deck the Halls," (which mentions the Yule log), and enjoy the whimsy and wonder of gazing into the flames.

Ancient tradition claims that saving some cooled embers to start your Yule log fire the following year will bring good fortune and, perhaps, even miracles into your home.

More Chicken Soup?

Many of the stories and poems you have read in this book were submitted by readers like you who had read earlier *Chicken Soup for the Soul* books. We publish at least five or six *Chicken Soup for the Soul* books every year. We invite you to contribute a story to one of these future volumes.

Stories may be up to twelve hundred words and must uplift or inspire. You may submit an original piece or something you clip out of the local newspaper, magazine, church bulletin or company newsletter. It could also be your favorite quotation you've put on your refrigerator door or a personal experience that has touched you deeply.

To obtain a copy of our submission guidelines and a listing of upcoming *Chicken Soup* books, please write, fax or check our Web site.

Chicken Soup for the Soul
P.O. Box 30880 • Santa Barbara, CA 93130
fax: 805-563-2945
www.chickensoup.com

Just send a copy of your stories and other pieces to the above address.

We will be sure that both you and the author are credited for your submission.

Supporting Others

In the virtuous spirit of giving, a portion of the proceeds from *Chicken Soup for the Soul: The Book of Christmas Virtues* will be donated to Vintage Voices, Inc.

Vintage Voices, Inc., is a growing nonprofit founded for the sole purpose of investing in a nearly forgotten and highly underserved segment of every community: the frail elderly.

Committed to fostering dignity, enthusiasm and socialization in long-term care facilities, Vintage Voices serves adult day cares, skilled nursing units, assisted living centers and nursing homes. Its monthly, multidisciplinary arts program, Silver Linings for Golden Agers, is designed specifically to stimulate socialization, rekindle dormant mental powers, restore confidence and encourage new enthusiasm.

Elderly residents participate in engaging, lively presentations—a merry mix of music, games, tactile aids, storytelling and reminiscing. Each thematic program is designed for active participation and involvement, specifically reaching those with multiple disabilities.

To learn more about this model agency, contact:

Vintage Voices, Inc.
1127 Garfield Avenue
Loveland, CO 80537
Phone: 970-669-5791

Who Is Jack Canfield?

Jack Canfield is one of America's leading experts in the development of human potential and personal effectiveness. He is both a dynamic, entertaining speaker and a highly sought-after trainer.

He is the author and narrator of several bestselling audio and videocassette programs, including *Self-Esteem and Peak Performance, How to Build High Self-Esteem, Self-Esteem in the Classroom* and *Chicken Soup for the Soul—Live.* He is regularly seen on television shows such as *Good Morning America, 20/20* and *NBC Nightly News.* Jack has co-authored numerous books, including the *Chicken Soup for the Soul* series, *Dare to Win* and *The Aladdin Factor* (all with Mark Victor Hansen), *100 Ways to Build Self-Concept in the Classroom* (with Harold C. Wells) and *Heart at Work* (with Jacqueline Miller).

Jack is a regularly featured speaker for professional associations, school districts, government agencies, churches, hospitals, sales organizations and corporations. His clients have included the American Dental Association, the American Management Association, AT&T, Campbell's Soup, Clairol, Domino's Pizza, GE, ITT, Hartford Insurance, Johnson & Johnson, the Million Dollar Roundtable, NCR, New England Telephone, Re/Max, Scott Paper, TRW and Virgin Records. Jack is also on the faculty of Income Builders International, a school for entrepreneurs.

Jack conducts an annual eight-day Training of Trainers program in the areas of self-esteem and peak performance. The program attracts educators, counselors, parenting trainers, corporate trainers, professional speakers, ministers and others interested in developing their speaking and seminar-leading skills.

For further information about Jack's books, tapes and training programs, or to schedule him for a presentation, please contact:

The Canfield Training Group
P.O. Box 30880 • Santa Barbara, CA 93130
Phone: 805-563-2935 • Fax: 805-563-2945
Visit our Web site: *www.chickensoup.com*

Who Is Mark Victor Hansen?

Mark Victor Hansen is a professional speaker who, in the last twenty years, has made more than four thousand presentations to more than two million people in thirty-two countries. His presentations cover sales excellence and strategies; personal empowerment and development regardless of stages of life; and how to triple your income and double your time off.

Mark has spent a lifetime dedicated to his mission of making a profound and positive difference in people's lives. Throughout his career, he has inspired hundreds of thousands of people to create a more powerful and purposeful future for themselves while stimulating the sale of billions of dollars worth of goods and services.

Mark is a prolific writer and has authored *Future Diary, How to Achieve Total Prosperity* and *The Miracle of Tithing*. He is coauthor of the *Chicken Soup for the Soul* series, *Dare to Win* and *The Aladdin Factor* (all with Jack Canfield), *The Master Motivator* (with Joe Batten) and *Out of the Blue* (with Barbara Nichols).

Mark has also produced a complete library of personal empowerment audio and videocassette programs that have enabled his listeners to recognize and use their innate abilities in their business and personal lives. His message has made him a popular television and radio personality, with appearances on ABC, NBC, CBS, HBO, PBS and CNN. He has also appeared on the cover of numerous magazines, including *Success, Entrepreneur* and *Changes*. In 2000, Mark was a recipient of the prestigious Horatio Algier Award for his humanitarianism.

Mark is a big man with a heart and spirit to match—an inspiration to people of all ages who seek to better themselves.

For further information about Mark write to:

MVH & Associates
P.O. Box 7665
Newport Beach, CA 92658
Phone: 949-759-9304 or 800-433-2314
Fax: 949-722-6912
Web site: *www.chickensoup.com*

Who Is Carol McAdoo Rehme?

No matter which hat she's wearing—dedicated writer and editor, nonprofit director, or public speaker—Carol McAdoo Rehme peppers everything she does with an enthusiasm for the power of story.

An active freelancer who has found her niche in the inspirational market, Carol is a prolific contributor to the *Chicken Soup* series. Her work also appears widely in other anthologies. In addition, Carol edited *Chicken Soup for the Bride's Soul, Chicken Soup for the African American Soul,* and *Chicken Soup for the Mothers of Preschoolers Soul.*

Besides coauthoring several gift books, she occasionally writes for magazines and some children's publications. *Chicken Soup for the Soul: Book of Christmas Virtues* is her first project to coauthor for *Chicken Soup.*

When she isn't busy writing stories, Carol is actively telling them. She presents at educational and corporate conferences and a variety of other venues including museums, dude ranches, libraries, schools, and civic clubs. As the Traveling Storyteller for the Loveland Public Library, Carol directed a park outreach program for ten years, serving thousands of children each summer.

Her current passion revolves around the frail elderly. Carol directs a vibrant nonprofit agency—Vintage Voices, Inc.—whose primary program, Silver Linings for Golden Agers, targets residents of long-term care facilities. This grant-driven arts model provides engaging thematic activities that are interactive and energetic, with a strong focus on sharing stories.

Kansas transplants, Carol and her husband, Norm, claim deep roots in Colorado where they raised their four children—Kyle, Katrina, Kayla and Koy. Carol now proudly wears new hats that read: Mother-in-law and Grammy.

She can be reached at:

Carol McAdoo Rehme
1127 Garfield Avenue
Loveland CO 80537
Phone: 970-669-5791
Web site: *www.rehme.com*
E-mail: *carol@rehme.com*

Contributors

Several of the stories in this book were taken from previously published sources, such as books, magazines and newspapers. These sources are acknowledged in the permissions section. However, some of the stories were written by humorists, comedians, professional speakers and workshop presenters, as well as by kids. If you would like to contact them for information on their books, audiotapes and videotapes, seminars and workshops, you can reach them at the addresses and phone numbers provided below.

The remainder of the stories were submitted by readers of our previous *Chicken Soup for the Soul* books who responded to our requests for stories. We have also included information about them.

Toby Ann Abraham-Rhine is a part-time counselor, teacher and performing artist. She and her husband choose to live very simply in order to travel. They saved for years, sold all they had and went around the world with their three children. Readers may enjoy the journey through *A Brilliant Teacher* from Sawtooth Press.

Kathryn Beisner is a writer and motivational storyteller. Her love of history and family traditions are celebrated in her popular audio book *Ordinary Women with Extraordinary Spirit!* and an by essay in *Chili Today, Hot Tamale.* Kathryn lives by the motto, "No Guts, No Story!" For more adventures visit *www.kbsproductions.com.*

Robert H. Bickmeyer is retired from General Motors. He writes for the Olive Branch Press, the Think Club and *Military Magazine,* as well as guest columns for newspapers in southeast Michigan. He is now writing a book, *Laughter in Real Life.* Bob plays senior citizen softball, volleyball and golf. He can be reached at (248) 879-0207.

Henry Boye is a professional writer/author/cartoonist whose work has appeared in many leading newspapers and magazines. He resides with his wife, Anita, in an adult community in Englishtown, New Jersey.

Ann K. Brandt writes magazine articles and essays. Her first book, *Learning to Walk Again,* tells of her experience with Guillain-Barré. She is working on *Facing Brain Cancer with Hope,* a book for anyone affected by cancer. Please e-mail her at *AnnGeoB@msn.com.*

Isabel Bearman Bucher, a retired teacher, has been writing, with no training, since 1984. She was raising teenagers, and saying it on paper with words seemed better than committing murder. She's published dozens of articles in many genres and has completed two books: *Nonno's Monkey: An Italian American Memoir*, and *Tweet Irene*, the story of a little house sparrow that lived with her family loosely for three years. She was a miracle. She and her husband, Robert, continue their honeymoon with life, changing homes throughout the world, walking mountains, finding adventures.

Pam Bumpus and husband, Alan, live near Charleston, Illinois. They have two wonderful daughters, a beautiful granddaughter and a brand new grandson. Pam writes as a hobby and enjoys sharing her stories. She can be contacted at *plbump@yahoo.com*.

Steve Burt's inspirational bestsellers include *A Christmas Dozen* and *Unk's Fiddle*. The Ray Bradbury winner *Odd Lot* won a Benjamin Franklin Award; *Even Odder* was runner-up to *Harry Potter* for the 2003 Bram Stoker Award (horror's top prize); *Oddest Yet* was a 2004 Stoker Finalist; *Wicked Odd* is his newest book. *www.burtcreations.com*.

Tamara J. Chilla was raised and educated in Oregon. She has traveled throughout the country working in sales and training for educational publishers. She has always been a stroyteller and currently is working on a series of children's books. Please e-mail her at *tamchilla@yahoo.com*.

Robin Clephane Steward is a stay-at-home mother of three. She lives in Indianapolis with her husband, Brian, two sons, a daughter and a lovable mutt named Boots. She enjoys Anne Perry novels, John Wayne movies and performing taxi service between her home and her local middle and high schools.

James Daigh has a bachelor's in creative writing/poetry. His careers have been in documentary and feature film production and publishing. His loves are: 1. his fantastic wife and inspiration, Marla; 2. poetry; 3. drawing and painting; 4. fine-art photography and this big, wide, beautiful world.

Mary Kerr Danielson began her writing career by joining a local writer's group at age fifty-something. (Known within a small circle of family and friends as the "Ditty Lady"—original verses for any and all obscure occasions—she's positive Hallmark isn't worried!) She and her husband, Kay, are parents of six daughters, one of whom is deceased. (After they all "left the nest," the nest was recently moved from Loveland, Colorado, to Riverdale, Utah.) Writing mainly about her life experiences, she also does poetry, plays and children's stories. E-mail her at *danielson_l@msn.com*.

Barbara "Binkie" Dussalt is a retired grandmother who enjoys her family, which includes her children Trudy, Susie and Jeff, her granddaughters, Aubrey Jessica and Michelle, and her great-grandchildren, Morgan, Troy and Max. She loves crafts, sewing and making her own expression cards.

Ellen Hamilton Fenter is a pastor, writer, counselor, community activist and blogger who currently enjoys life and ministry in El Paso, Texas. She is a mother and grandmother whose heart always longs for the serenity of her native land, New Mexico. Pastor Ellen's enduring passion is for "the least of these."

Nancy B. Gibbs is the author of four books, a weekly columnist for two newspapers and an editor. She has contributed to numerous anthologies and magazines. Nancy has had nineteen stories published in *Chicken Soup for the Soul* anthologies. She is a pastor's wife, mother and grandmother. Contact Nancy at *Daiseydood@aol.com* or *www.nancybgibbs.com*.

Angela Hall has been publisher/editor of a newspaper in Canada for twenty years. She has also edited several books, three of which were on the bestseller list. Angela is now retired and looking forward to devoting more time to writing letters of encouragement to sick and needy children as well as to survivors of cancer. You can reach her at *angel@belco.bc.ca*.

A lover of animals, both wild and tame, **Bonnie Compton Hanson** has authored or coauthored over twenty books, plus hundreds of poems and articles—including those in twelve *Chicken Soup* books.

Emily Sue Harvey's upbeat stories appear in women's magazines, *The Compassionate Friends* magazine, the *Chocolate* series, *Chicken Soup, From Eulogy to Joy* and *Caution: Children Praying*. Her two current completed novels are *God Only Knows* and *Sunny Flavors*. She writes to make a difference. Contact her at *emilysue1@aol.com*.

Armené Humber is a career coach who helps low-income clients recognize their potential and find their places in today's challenging workplace. She lives in Southern California, has a master's degree in Christian leadership from Fuller Theological Seminary and enjoys writing inspirational stories. Contact her at *armhumber@aol.com*.

Margaret Kirk has a master's from Gaddard College with graduate work in heart–centered counseling from the University of Santa Monica. She is currently a fiber artist, doll maker and the executive director of the Four Corners Child Advocacy Center in Colorado. Please e-mail her at *eurydice4@yahoo.com*.

Vickie Ryan Koehler received her bachelor of arts from Sam Houston State University in Huntsville, Texas, in 1979, and then studied for her master's degree in Spanish at the University of Kentucky. She presently resides in Liverpool, Texas, with her family and teaches in the Alvin Independent School District.

Margaret Lang received her bachelor of arts from Brown University in 1963. She teaches women and children's groups in California. Margaret has three published stories, two in *Chicken Soup for the Father and Daughter Soul*. Her daughter is a physician/missionary, her son a youth pastor, and she has two granddaughters.

Charlotte A. Lanham is a retired teacher and columnist. She is a frequent contributor to *Chicken Soup for the Soul.* Charlotte and her husband, Ray, cofounded a nonprofit organization called Abbi's Room Foundation, providing beds and bedding for children of Habitat for Humanity families. E-mail her at *charlotte.lanham@sbcglobal.net.*

Sharon Whitley Larsen, a former special-education teacher, has contributed previously to *Chicken Soup* books (4th, 5th, Teenage and Golden editions). Her work has also appeared in *Reader's Digest, Los Angeles Times Magazine* and other publications. She currently writes travel stories for Copley News Service and can be reached at *SWhittles@aol.com.*

Margaret R. Middleton has experienced miracles and unhappiness in her seventy-five years of life. God has been her foundation. She has written fifteen episodes of her childhood and, as an adult, a biography that readers will perceive as an adventurous experience of her life.

Sheila Myers's work has appeared in *Grit,* the *St. Anthony Messenger* and *Staying Sane When Your Family Comes to Visit* (due Fall, 2005). She ghosted Carmen's memoir, *Daughter of the Spirit: A Soul's Journey Home,* for which she seeks a publisher. Ms. Myers can be reached at *sjblomyers@sbcglobal.net.*

Edmund W. Ostrander holds a bachelor's of music from Oberlin Conservatory, a master's of education in music from C. W. Post College, a master's of education in counseling psychology from Cambridge College and a Ph.D. in humanities from the Union Institute. He has taught on every level and currently teaches storytelling for Cambridge College and Lesley University. E-mail him at *edostra@aol.com.*

Annette Seaver's greatest passion is mothering. She currently has eleven children: seven biological, four adopted and two "on hold." She's been to China and Saoma, and anticipates traveling to Mongolia soon. She mentors unwed mothers, organizes a variety of teen activities, volunteers at school and church, and enjoys writing.

Stephanie Welcher Thompson married her sweetheart, Michael, on February 14, 2002. These days, they enjoy family life in an Oklahoma City suburb with their darling two-and-a-half-year-old daughter, Micah. Reach them at P.O. Box 1502, Edmond, OK 73083, or *stephanie@stateofchange.net.*

Jim West is one of the most sought after cruise professionals in the travel industry. He is the author of four travel books and a contributing author in *Chicken Soup for the Traveler's Soul.* He was a professional cruise director for ten years; has sailed on over 850 cruises, including a cruise to Antarctica with Sir Edmund Hillary; visited over 72 countries around the world and is a popular international speaker. He has received his certification in Youth Ministry from the University in Stubenville, Ohio, and continues to minister to teens through a travel ministry. You can reach Jim at *www.TravelWest.com* or by calling (815) 878-3600.

Woody Woodburn is a sports columnist for the *Daily Breeze* in Torrance,

California. He has been honored for column writing by the Associated Press Sports Editors, appeared in *The Best American Sports Writing* anthology, is a frequent contributor to the *Chicken Soup* series and authored two books. He can be reached at *Woodycolumn@aol.com*.

Jane Zaffino recently retired from Bell Canada after thirty years of dedicated service. She is now pursuing her lifelong dream of writing by taking courses at George Brown College. She currently lives in Toronto with her husband of thirty years and their two children. You can reach Jane at *janezaffino@yahoo.ca*.